BARRON'S BOOK NOTES

STEPHEN CRANE'S

The Red Badge of Courage

BY
Elsa Dixler

SERIES EDITOR
Michael Spring
Editor, *Literary Cavalcade*
Scholastic Inc

D1607984

BARRON'S EDUCATIONAL SERIES, INC.

ACKNOWLEDGMENTS

We would like to acknowledge the many painstaking hours of work Holly Hughes and Thomas F. Hirsch have devoted to making the *Book Notes* series a success.

All inquiries should be addressed to:
Barron's Educational Series, Inc.
250 Wireless Boulevard
Hauppauge, New York 11788

Library of Congress Catalog Card No. 84-18441

International Standard Book No. 0-8120-3438-4

Library of Congress Cataloging in Publication Data
Dixler, Elsa.
   Stephen Crane's The red badge of courage.

   (Barron's book notes)
   Bibliography: p. 88
   Summary: A guide to reading "The Red Badge of Courage"
with a critical and appreciative mind encouraging analysis
of plot, style, form, and structure. Also includes
background on the author's life and times, sample tests, term
paper suggestions, and a reading list.
   1. Crane, Stephen, 1871–1900. Red badge of courage.
2. United States—History—Civil War, 1861–1865—
Literature and the war. [1. Crane, Stephen, 1871–1900.
Red badge of courage.   2. American literature—History
and criticism] I. Title. II. Series.
PS1449.C85R3925 1984   813'.4   84-18441
ISBN 0-8120-3438-4 (pbk.)

PRINTED IN THE UNITED STATES OF AMERICA

456   550   9876543

CONTENTS

HOW TO USE THIS BOOK

You have to know how to approach literature in order to get the most out of it. This *Barron's Book Notes* volume follows a plan based on methods used by some of the best students to read a work of literature.

Begin with the guide's section on the author's life and times. As you read, try to form a clear picture of the author's personality, circumstances, and motives for writing the work. This background usually will make it easier for you to hear the author's tone of voice, and follow where the author is heading.

Then go over the rest of the introductory material—such sections as those on the plot, characters, setting, themes, and style of the work. Underline, or write down in your notebook, particular things to watch for, such as contrasts between characters and repeated literary devices. At this point, you may want to develop a system of symbols to use in marking your text as you read. (Of course, you should only mark up a book you own, not one that belongs to another person or a school.) Perhaps you will want to use a different letter for each character's name, a different number for each major theme of the book, a different color for each important symbol or literary device. Be prepared to mark up the pages of your book as you read. Put your marks in the margins so you can find them again easily.

Now comes the moment you've been waiting for—the time to start reading the work of literature. You may want to put aside your *Barron's Book Notes* volume until you've read the work all the way through. Or you may want to alternate, reading the *Book Notes* analysis of each section as soon as you have finished reading the corresponding part of the original. Before you move on, reread crucial passages you don't fully understand. (Don't take this guide's analysis for granted—make up your own mind as to what the work means.)

Once you've finished the whole work of literature, you may want to review it right away, so you can firm up your ideas about what it means. You may want to leaf through the book concentrating on passages you marked in reference to one character or one theme. This is also a good time to reread the *Book Notes* introductory material, which pulls together insights on specific topics.

When it comes time to prepare for a test or to write a paper, you'll already have formed ideas about the work. You'll be able to go back through it, refreshing your memory as to the author's exact words and perspective, so that you can support your opinions with evidence drawn straight from the work. Patterns will emerge, and ideas will fall into place; your essay question or term paper will almost write itself. Give yourself a dry run with one of the sample tests in the guide. These tests present both multiple-choice and essay questions. An accompanying section gives answers to the multiple-choice questions as well as suggestions for writing the essays. If you have to select a term paper topic, you may choose one from the list of suggestions in this book. This guide also provides you with a reading list, to help you when you start research for a term paper, and a selection of provocative comments by critics, to spark your thinking before you write.

THE AUTHOR
AND HIS TIMES

When *The Red Badge of Courage* was published in 1895 (it first came out in installments in a Philadelphia newspaper at the end of 1894), the Civil War had been over for thirty years. In some ways Americans were forgetting the war. In the South, whites tried to undo some of the war's effects. By the 1890s many of the old Confederate leaders were back in power, and blacks had lost their right to vote, and couldn't go to school with whites. But in other ways Americans liked to remember the Civil War. In little towns in New England and the Middle West they built monuments to Civil War dead—something they had not done after the Revolution or the War of 1812. Stories about the war were tales of bravery and heroism. Its songs were stirring anthems like "The Battle Hymn of the Republic."

Imagine, then, how shocking it must have been to turn the pages of *The Red Badge of Courage*. Here was a novel where you didn't even find out the hero's name—if you could call a boy who ran away from battle a hero—until halfway through the book. Instead of being wounded by Confederate fire, this so-called hero gets his "red badge of courage" from a panicked fellow soldier. Henry Fleming's best friend, the tall soldier, Jim Conklin, dies horribly, jerking around alone in the middle of a field, rather than expiring decorously in Henry's arms with his mother's name on his lips. When Henry overhears a general speaking with his aide, he wants to know when he's getting his cigars, not about the progress of the battle. And as if it weren't enough that this Stephen Crane stripped away the glories of war, who had ever written in such language? Most novels were graced by flowing sentences, ample paragraphs, and chapters it took a whole evening to read. What was this? Who had ever heard anything as weird as Crane's language?

Those of us who watched "M*A*S*H" or read *Catch-22* are not shocked by Crane's vision of war. But readers in 1895 couldn't wait to find out who Stephen Crane was. One veteran insisted that Crane had been in his regiment at Antietam (one of the great battles of the Civil War). He was wrong. Stephen Crane was a twenty-four-year-old journalist who had never seen a battle, much less fought in one; a young man who had flunked out of two colleges, where he had displayed more talent for playing baseball and drinking beer than for writing. (Several years later, after Crane covered a war in Greece as a journalist, he confessed with relief to his friend, the English novelist Joseph Conrad, that *"The Red Badge of Courage* is all right.")

So how did a twenty-four-year-old who had never seen combat create a novel that would forever change the way Americans wrote about war? One answer might be that he copied the style of a European novelist. In fact, European writing in the 1890s was beginning to change in some exciting ways. Two French writers, Émile Zola and Gustave Flaubert, published novels that outraged proper people. Zola in particular wrote in a way that people found brutal and shocking. He wrote about prostitutes and coal miners, people who did not appear in the novels of the day. And he tried to show that people were in the grip of forces— heredity, environment, and instinct—that they could not control. Some modern critics have claimed that Zola's novel *La Débacle* was one inspiration for *The Red Badge of Courage*. Stephen Crane had read some of Zola's novels—in English, since his French wasn't that good—and he knew about *La Débacle*, although nobody knows for sure whether he read the novel or only a review of it. *War and Peace* and *Sebastapol*, both by the Russian novelist Leo Tolstoy, have also been named as possible sources for *The Red Badge of Courage*. Again, Crane may have read the books, but he also may have read only reviews.

Crane liked to read, and in high school he had enjoyed nineteenth-century British novels and the Greek and Roman classics. But he was always more interested in two other things: playing baseball and acting rowdy—drinking beer, playing cards, smoking, and swearing, all the things that would have made his minister father turn over in his grave. It doesn't seem likely that Stephen Crane would have been inspired by other people's books.

Baseball and being tough were probably what helped Crane imagine what war was like. In fact, Crane once said, "I believe that I get my sense of the rage of conflict on the football field. The psychology is the same." Actually, baseball was Crane's sport. He was an excellent player, and loved to show off by playing without a glove. Crane claimed that when he was at boarding school, a place called Claverack College on the Hudson River in New York State, "I never learned anything. But heaven was sunny blue and no rain fell on the diamond when I was playing baseball." When Crane went to college (despite its name, Claverack was a high school), first at Lafayette College in Easton, Pennsylvania, and then at Syracuse University in Syracuse, New York, the amount of time he spent playing baseball contributed to his flunking out.

Crane wasn't being fair to Claverack. He learned something there, something about being a soldier. For Claverack was a military academy, and Crane's mother had sent him there because the only thing he loved more than baseball was playing soldier. (Once, as a boy in Asbury Park, New Jersey, Crane had gotten so involved in a game of war that he buried a friend in the sand.) At Claverack Stephen practiced military drills. And in the evenings, around tables in the dining hall, the teachers, former soldiers, sometimes reminisced about their experiences in the Civil War. Stephen's favorite, General John Bullock Van Petten, had fought at Antietam, which the battle described in *The Red Badge of Courage* resembles in some ways (although it is closer to the battle of Chancellorsville in May 1863). Some of the stories that showed up in *The Red Badge of Courage* may have been planted in Stephen's head by General Van Petten's tales.

But in the end, Stephen Crane's ability to describe war and to get inside soldiers' heads probably came from the kind of person he was, and the way he had grown up. Stephen Crane was a minister's son—and a minister's grandson and nephew, too—and like at least some other boys in that position, he wanted to show people that he was a regular guy. That need may have led Stephen to a career in journalism (although both of his parents also wrote, as did two of his brothers), and to a desire to shock more respectable people.

The struggle to find out what he was really made of, and to test his courage in battle, was as important to Stephen Crane as it was to Henry Fleming. After

The Red Badge of Courage was published he traveled as a journalist to Cuba, then fighting for its independence from Spain, and to Europe, where he eventually settled in England. He became a respected war correspondent for several newspapers, showing a great deal of bravery, and he continued to write stories, novels, and poems. Like Henry, Stephen could have said that "He had been to touch the great death, and found that, after all, it was but the great death. He was a man." Stephen Crane died of tuberculosis on June 5, 1900, five months before his 29th birthday. If he had lived, would he have, as Henry did, "rid himself of the red sickness of battle" and "turned . . . with a lover's thirst to images of tranquil skies, fresh meadows, cool brooks"? It is hard to know. It's almost impossible to imagine Stephen Crane as an old man.

THE NOVEL

The Plot

The Red Badge of Courage describes how Henry Fleming, a young soldier from New York State, first experiences fighting at the Battle of Chancellorsville during the American Civil War. At first Henry is nervous, and even runs away after one of the first skirmishes, but eventually he returns to his regiment and fights bravely. By the battle's end, Henry has learned a lot about himself and the meaning of courage. He has grown up, and so have many of his fellow soldiers.

This is the plot of *The Red Badge of Courage*. The novel does not tell a story so much as it focuses on the perceptions and development of one young man. We see what war looks like to Henry, and the effect it has on his thoughts and feelings. In many chapters there is action—Henry's friend dies, or the Confederate soldiers charge and the Union troops push them back. But in other chapters nothing much happens except in Henry's mind. Because Henry's emotions swing back and forth—sometimes he feels proud and brave, other times like a criminal—the book does not follow a straight line either.

As *The Red Badge of Courage* opens, we meet Henry Fleming, who has signed up for the army against his mother's wishes, full of dreams of becoming a hero. But so far he has done nothing but sit around the camp. With all that time on his hands, Henry begins to worry whether he will be able to fight bravely, or whether he'll run away when the shooting starts. He talks to some of the others about it, but because he cannot really explain his fears, he feels more and more alone. Jim Conklin, a friend from home, thinks he'll do whatever the other boys do; a loud soldier named Wilson is full of boasts. The first sight of battle is terrifying, and Henry feels worse and worse. Even the loud soldier, convinced he's about to be killed, gives Henry some letters for his family.

During the first skirmish Henry fights well, feeling as much part of the regiment as the fingers of a hand. They hold the enemy back. But while they are relaxing, the enemy strikes again. Now Henry is exhausted and terrified. When two men standing near him turn and run, he throws down his gun and races to the rear. He tells himself that the regiment was about to be wiped out, and that saving himself was a responsible act. But he soon realizes that the line had held. Now he is furious at the other soldiers for making him look like a coward when he's sure that he was right.

Feeling awful, Henry walks into the woods, both to hide and to make himself feel better. He throws a pine cone at a squirrel, the animal scampers off, and he thinks to himself, "What I did was only the law of nature; animals protect themselves." But in the heart of the forest, under trees arched like a cathedral, Henry confronts a horrible sight: a dead man terribly decayed, whose face is covered with ants. He stares at the dead soldier, realizing that this is the real law of nature.

Leaving the woods, Henry walks along with some wounded men. He envies them and wishes that he too had a wound, a red badge of courage. One of the men, he realizes, is his friend, Jim Conklin, who is dying. Henry and another soldier, a tattered man, follow Jim into a field, where he runs from bush to bush, looking for a good place to die. Then, his body jerking horribly, he falls. This scene ends with the most famous line in the book: "The red sun was pasted in the sky like a wafer."

The tattered man keeps asking Henry where he's been wounded. His questions make Henry nervous that he'll be found out. So he leaves the tattered man—who is badly wounded and needs help—and goes on alone. Next he encounters some soldiers who appear to be retreating. Eager to find out what s going on, Henry grabs one soldier's arm. In a panic, the soldier hits Henry on the head with the butt of his rifle. Now Henry has a red badge of courage—except that it came from his own side! A man with a cheery voice comes along and helps Henry find his way back to his regiment, where the others welcome him warmly. They do not question his story, and believe that the top of his head was grazed by a cannonball. The loud soldier, Wilson, seems to have quieted down, and he and Henry become good friends. Henry feels a little superior to him because Wilson thought he would die in the first encounter, but he gives him back his letters without rubbing it in.

Henry is still struggling with himself. He's afraid he'll be found out, but he also feels pretty good, telling himself that at least he ran away bravely. When the next day's fighting begins, Henry gets so involved in shooting that he doesn't stop even when the rebels withdraw. During the next charge, some of the other soldiers hesitate, and Henry helps the lieutenant urge them forward. He sees the Union flag falling, and he and Wilson pull it out of the hands of the dying color bearer. After the next charge the regiment is criticized for returning to its lines too quickly, but Henry and Wilson are commended for bravery. They charge again, they're exhausted, but another charge is necessary. Unbelievably, they find some remaining strength and move forward in a frenzy, not thinking about danger or themselves. They win—Wilson captures the Confederate flag and they take prisoners.

During the actual fighting Henry had not been thinking about himself; he acted on instinct, feeling like an animal or a savage. As the regiment marched away, he began to think about his experiences. He was proud of his bravery—although it was nothing like his childhood dreams—and embarrassed by his desertion of the tattered man. But in the end he realized that through it all he had become a man. Walking along, he daydreamed about the comforts of peace as the sun broke through the heavy clouds.

The Characters

Henry Fleming

Henry Fleming is the major character in *The Red Badge of Courage*. Because Crane never tells us what he looks like, just how old he is, or exactly where he comes from, and usually refers to him as "the youth" or "the young soldier," Henry could be any young man experiencing war for the first time.

Yet even without these facts about Henry, we do know quite a bit about what he's like. We know that he grew up on a farm in New York State. His father is apparently dead, and he was raised by his loving mother. We know—from his mother's warning as she says good-bye to him—that his life has been pretty quiet and protected.

Henry signs up in the army because he is excited by the idea of being a hero. He has read in school about the ancient warriors (he knows that war is no longer like that), and he is thrilled by the sound of church bells in the night, sounding the news of victory. He doesn't think at all about the Union cause. He joins the army even though he knows that his mother wants him to stay on the farm, but he is a little apologetic when he tells her. We can see how immature Henry still is by how he feels about his mother's reaction to the news. She gives him hand-knitted socks and sensible advice; he wants a speech about heroism. But he does have a chance to play the hero when he visits his old school, and also on the train to Washington.

But these visions of glory sink quickly in the mud of camp life. Henry's regiment, the 304th New York, doesn't see any action for quite a while, and Henry is bored and uncomfortable. He is also insecure, and worries about whether he will really be as brave as he'd like to be. He tries to talk to some of the other soldiers—his friend Jim Conklin from back home, and a loud soldier named Wilson—but the others don't seem to be as apprehensive as he is, or at least they don't show it. He can't explain his fears clearly, so he doesn't get the reassurance he needs, and he feels frightened and alone.

Henry fights well enough in the regiment's first engagement with the enemy, but in the second he is exhausted and very scared. When two men standing near him run, he throws down his gun and races away from the fighting. He rationalizes his action by telling himself that the regiment was about to be wiped out. When he realizes that instead they had won, he becomes angry at his fellow soldiers. Now Henry's flight becomes emotional as well as physical. He is running away from what he has done.

During his flight, he has many important experiences. He comes upon a dead man in the woods, and he watches the death agonies of his friend Jim Conklin. When the tattered soldier questions him about his own wound, Henry runs away again. His discomfort at being found out is stronger than his feeling of responsibility for a dying man.

Being wounded by a retreating Union soldier is the beginning of a change in Henry. Until now he has been full of rationalizations and denial. He is afraid not only of battle, but of being teased by his fellow soldiers. When the panicked soldier strikes him on the head, Henry has a real wound to match his inner wound of fear and shame. (The tattered man had asked Henry whether he was wounded inside, and in a way the answer was yes.) Even though Henry's "red badge of courage" is phony, it helps him to feel and act like someone who has experienced war. As Henry begins to think about the previous day, he realizes that he has really seen a lot.

But Henry's achievement of courage and maturity isn't easy. Even after he is wounded, and finds his regiment again, he is full of poses and hot air. He tells the others a lie—that he was wounded while fighting with another regiment—and they believe him. By the next day he feels pretty good about himself, conveniently forgetting about the cowardly and irresponsible things he did. Henry is feeling so smug that he begins to criticize the generals and boast about his own heroism, until he is brought down a peg by one of the other soldiers.

When the regiment goes into battle on the second day, Henry stops thinking about himself and begins to act on instinct. Then he is able to fight bravely, even heroically. He is pleased with these real achievements, and enjoys being singled out for praise by the lieutenant and the colonel. When the fighting ends, and Henry has time to evaluate all of the events of the past two days, he is able both to take pride in his courage and to look at his cowardice realistically. Now, at last, he has become a man.

Some readers of *The Red Badge of Courage* disagree about Henry's character. Those readers who think that the book is a Christian allegory (that the red sun in the sky is a communion wafer and that Jim Conklin represents Jesus Christ) think that Henry is redeemed by Jim's death. Others, who see it as a psychological study of the effects of war on a young man, think that in human terms Henry has grown and matured, that he has given up his dreams of individual glory and learned the real meaning of courage, the giving up of selfishness. These readers see Henry's realistic evaluation of himself in Chapter 24 as proof of his development.

But some people think that Henry has not changed that much by the end of the book. They point out that there is no steady growth in Henry's understanding. Even after the horrible experiences of his day of flight, when he looked death in the face, he can still tell himself that he is braver than Wilson. These readers see Henry's feelings of love for the flag in Chapter 19 as silly romanticism. And they argue that after his experience in the forest in Chapter 7 he should know better than to fantasize about the beauty of nature, as he does at the book's end. To these readers, Henry's visions of the comforts of peace are daydreams every bit as boyish as his earlier thinking about war. Besides, the war is hardly over; it will continue for two more years.

Another dispute over Henry's character focuses on how much he is in control of what he does. Some readers see Henry as a creature of instinct throughout the book. He runs away out of instinct (he is tired, he sees two soldiers deserting), he returns to his regiment out of instinct, and eventually he fights bravely out of instinct. These readers point to the patterns of imagery in the novel to support their argument. Crane repeatedly describes war as a beast or a machine. Either way it is a force bigger than any one man. Henry himself thinks of the regiment as an iron box he's caught in, and as a hand of which he's one finger. He returns to the regiment like a moth to a flame. Henry's maturation, these people claim, is the same as the regiment's growth in experience; these things just happen. Heroism, they say, isn't individual; it's acting according to instinct within the regiment.

But other readers, while agreeing that Crane shows war to be a force larger than individual men, argue that Henry does make choices. He does not wind up winning the battle himself as he once dreamed he would. That kind of warfare no longer exists, if it ever did. But within the boundaries set down by the nature of the war and the regiment, Henry does reflect, and he does become, at least in part, responsible for his actions. This debate about Henry's character is part of a larger question about whether *The Red Badge of Courage* is really a naturalistic novel, that is, whether Crane sees people as being totally in the grip of forces outside themselves.

You must decide for yourself what you think about Henry's character. One way to do that is to pay close attention as you read the book to what is going on in Henry's mind. Remember that much of the vivid and unusual language in *The Red Badge of Courage* describes how things looked to Henry. He is thoughtful and observant, and we really do hear a lot about his reactions to things. You should also try to separate what

Stephen Crane thinks about Henry from what you might think. You can do that by listening carefully to the narrator's voice on the rare occasions when it describes characters or comments on the action.

Henry's Mother

Henry's mother is not an important character in the novel, and she disappears after Chapter 1. But we still learn something about her, and through her about Henry. She is hard working—she milks the cows, peels potatoes, knits socks, and makes blackberry jam. And she dearly loves her son.

Henry is annoyed because his mother won't see him as the hero he wants to be. And in fact, she does treat him as if he were a little boy. She warns him to stay away from bad company, not to do anything he couldn't tell her about, and not to drink or swear. And she tells him to send his socks back to her for darning.

At the same time, much of her advice is realistic and sensible. She doesn't want him to go to war, and she claims—probably correctly—that he'd be more useful on the farm. But it takes Henry the space of the whole novel to learn the truth of what his mother tells him— "Yer jest one little feller amongst a hull lot of others." His mother urges him to be brave—she tells him not to shirk, and to do what's right, even if it means being killed—but it's a more mature kind of bravery than Henry can understand at this point. When in Chapter 15 Henry imagined destroying his mother's "vague feminine formula for beloved ones doing brave deeds on the field of battle without risk of life," he wasn't being fair to her. His mother's only "feminine formula" is that women have to bear their men going off to war.

Jim Conklin

Jim Conklin, "the tall soldier," appears several times early in *The Red Badge of Courage*. In fact, he is the first character we meet, as he goes down to the river to wash his shirt in the muddy water. Jim returns to camp with a rumor that the army is about to move. Some of the men believe him, some men don't, but they all listen to him. Jim appears to be a natural leader.

Jim is always calm and matter-of-fact, even under difficult circumstances. Henry Fleming, his childhood friend, can't understand why Jim seems unconcerned about the coming battle when he, Henry, is so frightened. Jim was no different from him when they were growing up together, Henry thinks. He comes to the conclusion—and he's probably right—that the challenge of war has brought out the best in Jim.

As the regiment is marched from place to place before the fighting begins, Henry rants about the stupidity of the officers, and generally bounces off the walls. Jim sits quietly, following orders and accepting whatever happens. He frequently eats pork sandwiches from his knapsack, and looks to Henry as if he is communicating deeply with his food. Jim helps to calm his friend down.

But for all his unself-conscious bravery, Jim Conklin is badly wounded in the first day's battle. When Henry encounters him again, Jim is dying. He does not complain about his wounds, but begs Henry to get him out of the road so that he is not run over by the artillery wagons. Even in his agony, he has been wondering how Henry was doing. As death approaches, Jim runs into a field, looking from bush to bush for the place he wants to die. He pushes aside Henry's offers of help, and meets his death alone. His body jerking horribly, he falls. Another witness to his death, the tattered soldier, is impressed by Jim's bravery.

What are we to make of this quiet, modest, yet exceedingly brave man? Some readers identify Jim with Jesus Christ, and claim that his death absolves Henry of his sins of cowardice. They point to Jim's initials, J.C., the wounds in his hands and sides, like Christ's stigmata, and the appearance of the "red sun pasted in the sky like a wafer" when Jim dies. (For more on this identification, see the detailed discussion of Chapter 9.) Other readers see him simply as a saintly, mature man, at peace with himself and so able to face war.

Jim's character sheds some light on Henry's. Jim appears to grow as a result of the experience of war, and that leads us to believe that Henry, too, can. His consistent courage contrasts with Henry's cowardice. The brave and simple way Jim faces death makes a contribution to Henry's—and our—understanding of the meaning of courage. In addition, the horrible realism with which Crane describes his death shows the hollowness of romantic dreams of war.

Wilson

Wilson is called "the loud soldier" in the early chapters of *The Red Badge of Courage*, but later, when he teams up with Henry, he usually appears as "the friend." We first meet Wilson early in Chapter 1 when he picks a fight with Jim Conklin about Jim's story that the army is about to move. Wilson has no more information than Jim does, but he already knows it all.

As the regiment prepares for battle, Henry Fleming tries to find out whether Wilson shares his fears. The loud soldier boasts about how well he'll fight, and is sure he'll never run. He laughs at Henry and makes him feel much worse. But just before the first battle Wilson brings Henry some letters to give his family after his death, for Wilson is sure he's about to die. So much for bravery!

We don't see Wilson during the chapters describing Henry's flight. When we meet him again he's very different. Wilson is the sentry when Henry returns to his regiment, and Wilson greets him warmly, and tenderly bandages his wound. He doesn't take offense when Henry snaps at him, and he gives Henry his blanket to sleep under. Henry sees that Wilson has been transformed by his experience of battle, that he no longer takes himself so seriously, but has a quiet belief in his abilities. When Henry points out this change, Wilson laughs and says that he used to be quite a fool. Blushing, Wilson asks Henry to return his letters.

During the next battle, Wilson, now called "the friend," assumes something of Jim Conklin's role in calming Henry down when his nervousness takes the form of bad-mouthing the officers. Wilson fights bravely, always in the front of the line, and along with Henry, is singled out for praise. Wilson helps Henry rescue the Union flag when the color bearer is shot, and, in the last skirmish, captures the Confederate flag.

In the book's early chapters we see some similarities between Wilson and Henry. Wilson's way of coping with fear is different from Henry's: he's obnoxious, and he doesn't realize how scared he is, the way the more thoughtful Henry does. The character of Wilson shows us that Henry isn't the only untested soldier, isn't the only one with a problem about being brave. Wilson is apparently changed by the first day's battle.

As with Jim's increasing bravery, the change in Wilson suggests that Henry will mature as well. By the end of the book Wilson and Henry have become so much alike—fighting bravely together—that they almost seem to have become one character.

The Tattered Man

Henry encounters the tattered man when, fleeing from his regiment, he falls in with a group of wounded soldiers. The tattered man appears to be simple and innocent. When we first meet him he is listening to a sergeant with such awe that the sergeant begins to laugh at him. The tattered man is almost pathetically eager to make friends with Henry. Unfortunately for him, his questions about Henry's nonexistent wound scare the young soldier off.

The tattered man and Henry meet again in Chapter 9, when the tattered man helps him to take care of Jim Conklin. The tattered man is impressed by Conklin's bravery, but he is too unsophisticated to express his admiration in more than the simplest language (he calls Jim's death "funny"). He is extremely sympathetic to what he imagines to be Henry's wounds (and he's right that Henry has a "queer hurt" inside, although he doesn't know how right). He is uncomplaining about his own injury, and bravely insists that he isn't going to die. But Henry, afraid the tattered man will figure out that he's not wounded, leaves him, probably to die alone.

It is hard to know what to make of the tattered man. The constant reference to him as "tattered" almost suggests a clown, and his simplicity causes the sergeant in Chapter 8 to call him a "yokel." Still, the tattered man is brave, kind, and responsible to others. Henry's response to him shows the young soldier at his worst, and as a foil to Henry, he plays an important role in the novel. But it is a little hard to believe the tattered man is quite real. Henry, his mother, Wilson, and Jim Conklin are described in at least some realistic detail. Despite references to his two children, and to his wish for a warm bed and a bowl of pea soup, the tattered man does not seem to be a fully realized character.

The Cheery-Voiced Man

This character not only lacks a name, but Henry never even sees his face. Still, the cheery-voiced man, in guiding Henry back to his regiment, makes a contribution to the book. His skill at threading his way through the woods and among the patrols, and his easygoing calm, make him seem magical to Henry, and so to us. But he appears to be a perfectly ordinary man.

Bill Smithers

Bill Smithers is a very minor character, but he is an interesting one. In Chapter 2, before we know his name, someone steps on his hand, and he swears loudly. In Chapter 4 we learn that Bill went to the hospital with his so-called wound. But when the doctor threatened to cut off his three crushed fingers—presumably in order to scare Bill out of malingering—Bill wouldn't let him. The soldier who tells this story laughs at Bill, saying that he wasn't scared, oh no, just mad.

Bill Smithers is a figure of fun who often pops up in the regiment's conversations. In the heat of battle in Chapter 6, a tired soldier wishes that Bill Smithers had stepped on his hand instead of he on Bill's. And in the last chapter another soldier announces that Bill says that the hospital, which is shelled every night, is more dangerous than ten thousand battles.

Bill Smithers serves some important functions in the novel, although he doesn't appear after Chapter 2. He, like Henry, is only pretending to be wounded. But while Henry came back to the regiment after being hurt, Bill took advantage of his phony wound to sit out the rest of the war in the hospital. That tells us that Henry did have some choice, and makes us think that his return to his regiment showed some guts. But Henry was terrified of being thought a coward, while Bill Smithers doesn't seem to mind it. The men joke about him, but he is the author of the joke. This also contrasts with Henry's attitude.

Lieutenant Hasbrouck

Hasbrouck, the young lieutenant of the 304th regiment, is always swearing. He is also, without thinking about it, extremely brave. Unlike the other officers we see, who don't have much concern for the enlisted men, Hasbrouck defends his soldiers' performance and makes sure they get the recognition they deserve. Always at the head of his troops, uncomplaining when he is wounded, Hasbrouck is a real leader. He is a model of what Henry and Wilson will achieve by the novel's end.

Other Elements

SETTING

The Red Badge of Courage takes place in and around Chancellorsville, Virginia, during the course of several days in late April and early May 1863. Not that Crane tells us either of those things. He doesn't even tell us that Henry and his friends are fighting the Civil War, although we can guess that from the soldiers' blue and gray uniforms. A reader who knows Civil War history will recognize some details in the novel—the strategy of crossing the river and circling behind enemy lines, the pontoon bridges, the plank road—from accounts of the bloody Battle of Chancellorsville. But not until Henry says sarcastically in Chapter 16, "All quiet on the Rappahannock," the name of the river that flowed through Chancellorsville, are we absolutely certain of the setting. The battle took place on May 2–3, and the story begins several days earlier, in the Union Army camp.

Henry and his regiment fight in the fields, forest, and hills around Chancellorsville, and occasionally he notices a house or a farmer's horses tied to a fence. The natural beauty of the scenery is sometimes contrasted to the ferocity of war. But there is not much detailed description of the setting. These woods and hills could be anywhere, just as the battle could be anywhere. The lack of specific detail generalizes the story for us. This is not only, maybe not even, a story of the American Civil War, but about war in general.

THEMES

Courage

The central theme of the book is courage—what it is and how to get it. When the book opens, Henry Fleming thinks courage is displayed by storybook heroes, the knights and Greek warriors he read about in school. Despite his mother's warning that he can't fight the whole war alone, Henry thinks he will. That is what courage means to him. Once he joins the army, and sees how horrible war is, he becomes terribly frightened. He worries that he will be a coward.

A number of other characters in the novel show various types of courage. Hasbrouck, the young lieutenant, is always brave, always urging his men forward, and always sticking up for them. Jim Conklin, Henry's friend, is calm and collected, follows orders, and faces death with matter-of-fact dignity. Henry's mother shows courage, too, when she sends Henry off to war even though she loves him and needs his help on the farm, saying, "The Lord's will be done." And the tattered man, who is kind and uncomplaining despite his wounds, also shows a kind of courage.

But the courage that is prized in this book is courage in battle. Crane describes it as unthinking, savage, and almost more animal than human. "It is," Crane writes, "a temporary but sublime absence of selfishness." By the second day of battle Henry and Wilson have achieved this kind of courage, as has the rest of the regiment.

"The red badge of courage" referred to in the title is a wound. It is ironic, of course, that Henry is finally wounded by a retreating Union soldier, not by an advancing Confederate one. His wound is really a badge of shame, not of courage. But he and the other soldiers treat it as if it were a wound honestly gotten—and perhaps, in a way, it was. Henry's experiences during this first flight from battle eventually teach him a great deal about life and death. When Henry shows real courage in the second day's fighting, he is not wounded.

War

The theme of war is closely related to that of courage. Crane describes war with a realism unusual for his time. He gives us the boredom and mud of camp life, the repetitiveness of soldiers' conversations, the arrogance of the officers, the constant thunder of the guns. He also shows us war in its almost surrealistic horror. We see the dreadful deaths of Jim Conklin, Jimmie Rogers, and many unnamed men. Again and again we see bodies twisted into unbelievable positions. And we see the terrible randomness of war. There is no reason why a bullet strikes one man and not another.

When the novel opens, Henry has a romantic view of war, which events quickly poke holes in. Even at his most heroic, when he picks up the falling Union flag, there is a gruesome detail—he has to pry the flagpole out of the dying color bearer's hands. War turns out to be much grimmer than Henry ever imagined, just as courage turns out to be a matter of animal instinct rather than individual grace. Still, Crane seems to accept Henry's view that war takes the measure of a man, and he certainly believed that in his own life. Some modern writers about war, like Ernest Hemingway, would agree; others, like Joseph Heller, would not.

The Individual and Society

This is a less important, but still recognizable, theme in *The Red Badge of Courage*. Again and again Henry has to be told, "You can't fight this war alone." He imagines himself turning back hordes of gray soldiers. He always knows better than the generals. Becoming a real hero—and a man—for Henry requires becoming a better member of the group. He learns to follow orders without complaining, and he begins to feel like part of the regiment. When Henry was concerned about saving himself, he ran away. Only when he learns that he's one man among many is it possible for him to show courage.

Growing Up

In the course of *The Red Badge of Courage* Henry Fleming—and Wilson and Conklin—do a lot of growing up. The generalized setting and Crane's habit of not using the soldiers' names makes this a story about the effect of war on young men, not just about the effect of the Civil War on a few individuals. But in some ways the story is even more general than that. It is about overcoming fear, and learning to be brave; about giving up romantic dreams, and looking at the world as it really is. In this way *The Red Badge of Courage* is not just the story of how Henry Fleming became a man, but a story about growing up. In that respect it resembles many of the great classics of western literature, from the Greeks on.

STYLE

The language in *The Red Badge of Courage* is unusually important. The way things are described—that is, the way Henry Fleming sees them—tells us most of what we know about how Henry is growing and changing. Not that much actually happens in the book; Henry's changing perceptions are its main action.

Crane uses two styles in *The Red Badge of Courage*. One is the straightforward realism of the dialogue. Most of the characters in the book talk like country people, and their speech is reproduced accurately, dropping final *g*'s and *d*'s and using words like *yer* for *your.* But although the dialect is accurate, he leaves some things out. Crane never lets us hear his soldiers swearing—he only tells us that they do.

The book's other style is also realistic, but it is a special kind of realism. Crane usually does not tell us what a thing "really" was, but rather what it looked like to an observer, usually Henry Fleming. In the opening lines of the book, for example, the landscape didn't really change from brown to green, but the rising sun made the fields look green rather than brown. In the same way, campfires across the rivers are dragons, the marching army is a serpent; a line of guns are Indian chiefs at a powwow, because they look that way to Henry. Instead of giving us details about the characters, Crane simply gives us an impression of them—"the loud soldier," "the youth," "the tall soldier." It is like a line drawing rather than an oil painting.

Crane writes in short sentences and paragraphs, and generally uses a simple vocabulary. He usually turns to fancy words only when he is making fun of a character's pretentions.

POINT OF VIEW

The Red Badge of Courage is told in the third person; that is, the narrator says "he," not "I." Someone other than Henry Fleming is telling this story, but it is still Henry Fleming's story. Henry is present in every chapter, and most chapters are about him (those that aren't are about his observations of other characters). So we can say that the novel's point of view is that of Henry Fleming.

Events in the book are described as they appeared to Henry. This technique is very effective in the battle scenes. The narrator may have read books about the Civil War, and known what was really going on, but Henry didn't. Because we see only what Henry saw, we get a very vivid view of war, with exploding shells, puffs of smoke, the screams of the wounded, and the constant noise of the guns. The chaos and confusion of war are presented through this focus on sometimes confusing details, and the short paragraphs add to the confusion.

But Henry Fleming is the only character we know from the inside. We know what he is thinking and feeling at every minute—even the weather changes with his moods! But we never find out what is going on in the minds of Jim Conklin or Lieutenant Hasbrouck or Wilson. Some readers have said that these other characters become almost extensions of Henry's personality. They are in the novel to provide comparisons and contrasts with Henry, but unlike him, they are not real people.

The narrator rarely says anything in his own voice. During Henry's flight, for example, we are inside Henry's head, seeing the dragon approach, and we understand why he runs. We also understand his rationalization and experience his shame and guilt. Sometimes the narrator makes a little fun of characters, as when he tells us in the first chapter that the tall soldier "developed virtues and went resolutely to wash a shirt." This comment does not tell us what Jim looked like, but gives the narrator's opinion of him. The narrative voice tells us what it thinks only a few times. The most important of these is in Chapter 19, when it defines courage as "a temporary but sublime absence of selfishness." This isn't the way Henry

Fleming talks or thinks, but he would probably agree with the definition.

FORM AND STRUCTURE

The Red Badge of Courage consists of twenty-four brief chapters; except for the first, longer one, they are all about the same length. Each chapter has an easily identifiable subject and a clear bearing on Henry's acquisition of courage and coming to manhood.

Readers like to divide the chapters into sections according to their theme. The only problem is that everyone likes to do it a different way. Do the four sections consist of chapters 1–6, 7–12, 13–18, and 19–24? Or does it make more sense to talk about chapters 1–4, 5–6, 7–11, 12–14, and 15–24? Or how about chapters 1–3, 4–8, 9–15, 16–20, and 21–24? Any way of dividing up the chapters that makes the book's meaning clearer to you makes sense.

A number of readers have pointed out that the chapters alternate in various ways. The army marches forward in some, and waits in others; the soldiers alternately charge and rest. This gives the book a kind of seesaw rhythm. Another reader claims that the chapters alternate between hope and despair in Henry's mind.

The Story

CHAPTER 1

Have you ever imagined that you were a hero— running into a burning house to rescue a child, racing after a mugger and getting someone's wallet back, or walking on the moon? Have you ever read about great battles of the past, like Iwo Jima or the Normandy landings, and pictured yourself fighting in them? Have you ever thought to yourself that there really isn't any way to be a hero anymore? And have you ever worried that you might not have what it takes to be truly brave?

Then meet Henry Fleming, a farm boy from upstate New York in the 1860s. Henry wants to be a hero and he isn't sure he's got the guts. To find out, he enlists in the Union army during the American Civil War. *The Red Badge of Courage* is his story. As you read the book, you will find yourself asking, along with Henry, what courage means, who has it, and how you get it.

The Red Badge of Courage opens like a movie: the camera pans to take in the whole scene. Spread over a range of hills are the tents and campfires of an army camp. As the camera turns, we see the color of the fields begin to change from brown to green, the fog lifts, and we hear the first noises in the camp. It is morning. We guess that it is spring, because the roads are ribbons of mud.

Now the camera focuses on a man who walks down to the muddy river at the bottom of the hill to wash a shirt and returns waving it above his head like a flag. This man, identified only as "the tall soldier," has something to tell the rest of the men. He has heard a rumor that the army is about to move, that the soldiers will cross the river and attack the enemy from the rear.

As the tall soldier delivers his news, some of his buddies begin to argue with him. One of them, "the loud soldier," shouts, "It's a lie!"

NOTE: Crane does not immediately tell us the names of the characters in *The Red Badge of Courage*. They are referred to as the tall soldier, the young soldier, the loud soldier. This makes us think that this is a story about kinds of people rather than specific people, that it is about any young soldier, not just this one.

As we, the readers, watch and listen to this argument, we pick up a number of facts. First we learn that the army has been camped in this place for a long time. The loud soldier says that he's gotten ready to move eight times so far, but they haven't moved yet. Then we learn that nobody has been telling these soldiers what's really going on, so they are trying to figure it out for themselves. That is why they are so dependent on rumors like the tall soldier's; even if they aren't true, they're all the information these men have. Finally we learn who the men are. They are soldiers of the Union (northern) army, because they wear blue shirts; and from their accents we can tell that many of them grew up in the country.

One of the men leaves the group and goes into his tent to lie down and think about what he has just heard.

NOTE: We still don't know the young soldier's name, but we know a lot about what his tent looks like! Crane tells us about the pictures on the walls, the cracker-box furniture, and the way the sunlight comes through the small window to make a square on the floor. And the way the soldiers talk—dropping the final *d*'s and *g*'s from their words, using words like *ain't*—is the way country people really sounded in the 1860s.

It's hard to believe that they are finally going into battle. As a boy, he had dreamed about war and had imagined himself a hero. But he had also come to believe that the time of the great wars was as far away as kings and castles. People would never again fight the way they had in the olden days.

NOTE: The fancy language Crane uses to describe the young soldier's daydreams—"He could not accept with assurance an omen that he was about to mingle in one of those great affairs of the earth"—is very different from his usual short sentences and matter-of-fact way of putting things. Here Crane is poking a little fun at the young soldier's fantasies about being a hero.

When the Civil War had started, the boy had wanted to enlist. His mother had discouraged him, saying that his work on the farm was more important than what he would do in the army. But he had probably thought that the army would be more exciting than milking the cows. Lying on his bunk in the tent, the young soldier remembers how he had signed up. One night at home he had listened excitedly as the church bells rang out the news of a great battle. When he went to his mother's room to tell her he was going to enlist, she replied, "Henry, don't you be a fool," and pulled her quilt over her head. This scene shows us that Henry's mother doesn't take him very seriously, and that she still treats him like a child. It also lets us know the young soldier's name—Henry.

But the next day Henry had enlisted anyway.
When he got home his mother was milking a cow. A
little hesitantly, he told her the news. "The Lord's will
be done, Henry," she sighed. But Henry was disap-
pointed by his mother's response. Although she cried
a little, she continued to go about her chores. And the
advice she gave him was as down-to-earth as milking
the cow. "I know how you are, Henry," she said, and
she told him not to "go a-thinkin' you can lick the hull
rebel army at the start, because yeh can't. Yer jest one
little feller amongst a hull lot of others. . . ." She
warned him against falling in with a bad crowd and
not to do anything "that yeh would be 'shamed to let
me know about. Just think as if I was a-watchin'
yeh." But at the same time she urged him not to shirk
and to do "what's right." Finally she gave him eight
pairs of socks, some shirts, and a glass of blackberry
jam. He is to send the socks back to her for repairs.

His mother's attitude—resigned, homey, still not
taking him entirely seriously—almost spoils Henry's
mood. He had hoped that she would say good-bye to
him like mothers did in history books. But as he
turned back for a last glimpse of home, he saw her
sobbing as she peeled potatoes, and he felt ashamed
of what he had done. Still, he had other chances to
feel excited. He stopped by his school, where a dark-
haired girl he liked stood at the window, watching
him leave. And on the train to Washington, the new
soldiers had been treated like heroes.

But life at camp had been disappointing. Henry
and his fellow recruits had nothing to do but sit
around and try to keep warm. He began to return to
his old idea that the time for heroic warfare was past,
and that he and his fellows were only part of "a vast
blue demonstration." The only Confederates he saw

were soldiers across the river, with whom the Union soldiers talked comfortably while they were all on guard duty at night.

The older soldiers liked to tease Henry and the others, calling them "fresh fish." They were full of stories of the horrors of war. But it was hard for Henry to know whether or not to believe them. Lying on his bunk, realizing that he was finally about to enter his first battle, he wondered whether he had the guts for it. "It had suddenly appeared to him that perhaps in a battle he might run. He was forced to admit that as far as war was concerned he knew nothing of himself."

Now the tall soldier, the one who had started the rumor that they were on the verge of fighting, and the loud soldier who had disagreed with him, come into the tent, still squabbling. Henry asks the tall soldier, whose name turns out to be Jim Conklin, whether any of the boys will run once the fighting starts. Jim thinks that some of them might, but that even though they are untested, the boys will do all right. Then Henry asks Jim the really hard question: "Did you ever think you might run yourself, Jim?" "If a whole lot of boys started and run, why, I s'pose I'd start and run," Jim answers. "But if everybody was a-standing and a-fighting, why, I'd stand and fight." Jim's answer makes Henry feel better, because it shows him that not everyone else is a storybook hero, either.

In this first chapter we meet people with different attitudes toward war. Henry imagines himself as a legendary hero like the ones he has read about, and likes to show off to the girls at school, but at the same time he is terrified that he will run at the first sign of fighting. The old veterans like to scare the new recruits with their war stories, making themselves seem brave. Henry's mother doesn't think much of war, and urges Henry to take care of himself and not to try to fight the whole Rebel army himself. Jim's idea is something like Henry's mother's —he sees himself as part of a group of soldiers. He isn't worried about individual courage. What they do, he will do; what they can't, he won't. Notice the behavior of the loud soldier. Why does he keep quarreling with Jim? Perhaps, even if he doesn't say so, he's a little frightened himself.

Crane introduces another theme of the book when he has Henry admit that "as far as war was concerned he knew nothing of himself." In the chapters that follow, Henry will learn what war is like, and will learn something about the meaning of courage; he will also learn what kind of person he is.

This first chapter also reveals quite a bit about Crane's style. In general, he writes in short sentences, paragraphs, and chapters, and his vocabulary is fairly simple, except when he is laughing at one of the characters. He shows us many realistic details of camp life; still, some of the descriptions of the scene are rather poetic, such as the opening paragraph. In reading *The Red Badge of Courage*, pay close attention to Crane's language. Where is he being poetic and using unusual metaphors? Where is he being realistic and giving us the details of daily life? Where is he being abstract and making the story seem like a fable? Crane's language communicates a great deal of meaning.

CHAPTER 2

As it turned out, Jim Conklin's rumor was wrong, and the regiment stayed where it was. This left Henry more time to worry about whether he would be brave enough to fight, and he began to feel increasingly isolated. He had known Jim Conklin, the tall soldier, since childhood. He didn't think that Jim could do anything that he, Henry, couldn't, and Jim didn't seem to be afraid of battle. But that didn't make him feel any better. Afraid to confess his fears openly to the other soldiers, he could not get the comfort that he needed from them.

Finally one morning the regiment prepared to move. As the men waited eagerly, a man on horseback rode up to the colonel. Were these the regiment's orders? As the messenger galloped off, he called to the colonel, "Don't forget that box of cigars!" Once again, Henry feels let down. The messenger and the colonel are concerned about the details of everyday life, not with heroism. They are very much like Henry's mother.

As the regiment marches along, the men begin to feel that they are all in this together. They sing songs and make jokes. When a fat soldier tries to steal a horse from a house they pass, and a young girl runs after him and rescues the animal, everyone cheers her and laughs at the soldier. The more the other soldiers form a group, the more Henry feels like an outsider.

Henry starts a conversation with the loud soldier, whose name, we find out, is Wilson. In reply to Henry's persistent questions, Wilson says, "I s'pose I'll do as well as the rest. . . . I'm not going to skedaddle." "You ain't the bravest man in the world, are you?" asks Henry, who is feeling very uneasy. "No, I ain't," the loud soldier answers. "I said I was going to do my share of fighting—that's what I said. And I am, too. Who are you, anyhow? You talk as if you thought you was Napoleon Bonaparte." We know very well that Henry doesn't feel like Napoleon, but we can see why he sounds that way. Henry is trying to make himself feel better about his own doubts, and he winds up insulting the loud soldier. After this discussion, Henry feels even worse.

NOTE: Henry is doing something that everybody does sometimes. He feels different from everybody else, but because he's embarrassed to tell people why, he sounds too sure of himself. He winds up feeling very much alone and very sorry for himself.

Crane's description of the army's preparations for its march is striking. In the opening paragraph of Chapter 1 Crane had referred to the "red, eyelike gleam of hostile campfires." Now he tells us that: "From across the river the red eyes were still peering." This is the beginning of a practice Crane follows throughout the novel, referring to inanimate objects as if they were alive. For example, the regiment, finally on the move, "was now like one of those moving monsters wending with many feet. . . . There was an occasional flash and glimmer of steel from the backs of all these huge crawling reptiles. From the road came creakings and grumblings as some surly guns were dragged away." The army has become a crawling reptile, and the guns have taken on human emotions. Later, when the army pitches its new camp, "Tents sprang up like strange plants. Campfires, like red, peculiar blossoms, dotted the night." The effect of all this is to make the army seem to be part of nature, subject to forces larger than itself. It also heightens the impression that we have already gotten from the use of labels like "the tall soldier" and "the young soldier," that this is not so much a story about a specific regiment from New York State in the American Civil War as it is a timeless story.

Crane also uses these dramatic visual images to help us understand what is going on inside Henry's mind. In a paragraph that begins, "One morning, however, he [Henry] found himself in the ranks of his prepared regiment," Crane tells us that "In the eastern sky there was a yellow patch like a rug laid for the feet of the coming sun; and against it black and patternlike, loomed the gigantic figure of the colonel on a gigantic horse." Later, "As he looked all about him and pondered upon the mystic gloom. . . . Staring once at the red eyes across the river, he conceived them to be growing larger, as the orbs of a row of dragons advancing. He turned toward the colonel and saw him lift his gigantic arm and calmly stroke his mustache."

Crane is again making inanimate objects human; the sun has feet that will step on the rug of a patch of sky. But here some of the personification is Henry's. He sees the enemy campfires as eyes, and imagines them as the eyes of approaching dragons. He also sees the colonel on his horse as "gigantic." Chances are, the colonel was no larger than any other man. As Henry observes him, silhouetted against the rising sun, we can both see the colonel in our own minds' eyes, and we can see Henry's vision of him as an enormous heroic figure. How disillusioning, then, when this gigantic figure, almost like a statue, turns out to be worrying over a box of cigars! Although the story is being told by a narrator, not by Henry, we are learning quite a lot about what is going on in Henry's mind. Henry is not saying to us, "I looked across the river," as he would if this were a first-person narrative. But instead of just telling us that Henry was afraid, or that Henry wanted to believe that war was heroic, Crane is letting us see the world through Henry's eyes. Through these images he shows us what Henry sees, and that helps us understand what Henry feels. In this chapter we recognize that the focus of the book will be on Henry and his perceptions. As the chapter ends we see through Henry's eyes again. He imagines his fear as a monster with many tongues, and "He admitted that he would not be able to cope with this monster."

CHAPTER 3

As this chapter opens, the army crosses the river on pontoon bridges, just as General Burnside's troops crossed the Rappahannock in order to attack Lee and Jackson's troops from the rear. The next day they woke early and marched deep into a forest. Hot and tired, they began to drop their knapsacks and take off some of their clothing, stripping down to what was absolutely necessary. Now they looked less like a new regiment.

Then the regiment camped again, and Henry began to think again that they were "a blue demonstration," there only to look like an army. But one morning the young soldier sensed that "the time had come. He was about to be measured." Looking around, he realized that he could not escape. The regiment "inclosed him. And there were iron laws of tradition and law on four sides. He was in a moving box." It seemed to him that he had not enlisted voluntarily, that he had somehow been forced into the army.

As the soldiers climbed a hill, they heard the sound of artillery. The young soldier scrambled to the top, expecting to see a battle scene spread out below him. Instead there was chaos. Henry and his regiment came upon the body of a dead soldier, and separated to walk around him. The boy lay on his back, his feet sticking out of his worn shoes. Death had exposed the poverty that the soldier may have been able to hide from his friends. Henry stared at the dead man, trying to find the answer to his big question about war.

The regiment halted in the forest, where some of the men began to build fortifications, but soon they were ordered to withdraw. The youth grumbled loudly as they marched from place to place for no reason that they could see. He still wished that things would be decided one way or another, that they would either return to camp or go into battle. He complained to the tall soldier, who sat calmly, eating a pork sandwich. Unlike the young soldier, the tall soldier seemed to accept whatever happened.

As the soldiers watched another brigade go into action ahead of them, the loud soldier approached the young one. Even though he had told the young soldier (in an earlier chapter) that he could fight as well as the rest, his lip was trembling as he said, "It's my first and last battle, old boy." Convinced that he was about to be killed, he gave the young soldier a small bundle of letters to bring to his family.

In this chapter, as the regiment prepares to go into battle, we see three reactions among the soldiers. Henry, the young soldier, continues to be agitated and upset. He still holds on to his romantic dreams, even though they are contradicted by what he observes. He alternates between wishing for battle and wishing to be back at camp or on the farm. The tall soldier, Jim Conklin, is quiet and resigned. And the loud soldier, Wilson, has a premonition of his death, and sentimentally gives the young soldier some papers to bring back to his folks. Which of them will show courage in the battle ahead? How would you act in their places?

Crane continues to employ symbolic language. Tracing some of the symbols from chapter to chapter will help us to understand Crane's meaning. One of the most important symbols in this book is color. We have already noticed references to campfires as "red eyes" or "red, peculiar blossoms." In this chapter war is described as a "red animal," and the skirmishing soldiers Henry views from the hill are called red, although their uniforms must have been blue. Yellow appears again in the color of the dead man's suit, and purple in the color of the soldiers' uniforms as they crossed the bridge in the early morning light. Be alert to color as it appears in the chapters that follow.

Color is not the only image Crane uses. Throughout these first three chapters he has made several references to Greek mythology. Henry, as a schoolboy, had dreamed about war as a "Greeklike struggle," and he had hoped that his mother would say something about returning on his shield, the way Greek warriors killed in battle were carried home. Often the images of Greek culture are used ironically—they represent Henry's fantasies of war, not the real thing. But it is interesting that at the opening of this chapter the Rappahannock (we still do not know its name) is characterized as "wine-tinted." Homer often referred in *The Iliad* to the "wine dark sea," and this allusion would have been easily recognized by Crane's readers at the time. Is Crane suggesting here that the Union soldiers really were as heroic as the Greek warriors of old?

Another frequent image in *The Red Badge of Courage* is religious. We have already heard about the "mystic gloom" of the morning and of the "weird, satanic effect" of firelight. In this chapter there are references to the "blood-swollen god" (of war) and to the "cathedral light" of the forest. The loud soldier waves good-bye to Jim in a "prophetic" manner. Religious imagery is another pattern that should be followed, especially when it relates to the tall soldier, Jim Conklin.

CHAPTER 4

The soldiers are poised on the edge of battle, trying to see through the smoke to figure out which way to point their guns. There is gossip about how other regiments and commanders are doing. "That young Hasbrouck, he makes a good off'cer. He ain't afraid 'a nothin'."

One of the soldiers tells a comic story about someone named Bill: "Bill wasn't scared either. No, sir! It wasn't that. . . . He was jest mad, that's what he was." Bill's hand had been trampled during the march (an episode we heard about in Chapter 2). Bill announced that he was willing to give his hand to his country (an ironic echo of Nathan Hale's "I only regret that I have but one life to lose for my country"), but left the battle to go to the hospital anyway. When the doctor threatened to amputate the three crushed fingers, Bill fought with him and stormed out.

As the young soldier and the others watch, the regiment ahead of them is being defeated. Shells whistle by, leaves fall from the trees, and wild yells are heard. Through it all, the veterans continue to joke. The lieutenant of the young soldier's company is shot in the hand. He swears so angrily that the men laugh. He holds the hand carefully so that the blood doesn't drip on his pants, and the captain helps him to wrap the wound in a handkerchief.

In this chapter as in the last we see a variety of kinds of courage. Some of the commanders the troops gossip about are said to have it. The soldier named Bill apparently does not; the comment that he wasn't scared, just mad at the doctor, seems to be sarcastic. For all his boasting, Bill wasn't willing to give up his hand. We also see the reaction of the lieutenant to the wound in his hand. This is the young soldier's first real view of battle, and it is wild and frightening.

As the young soldier's regiment is surrounded by troops fleeing the battle they have just lost, he looks fearfully at their faces. Now it is up to the reserves, his own group. He has not yet seen the monster that drove his troops away, but he expects to, and then, he thinks, he really might run himself.

CHAPTER 5

In this chapter the young soldier participates in a battle for the first time. The 304th regiment, to which he belongs, stands firm. Yet the battle itself is more horrible than anything that we, or the young soldier, have seen yet.

As the Confederate troops suddenly appeared, the young soldier tried to remember whether his rifle was loaded. He heard a general shout savagely to the colonel of the 304th, "You've got to hold 'em back!" while the colonel stammered, "we-we'll d-d-do—do our best, General."

Perspiration streaming down his face, his mouth slightly open, the young soldier began to fire his gun. Then "He suddenly lost concern for himself. . . . He became not a man but a member. . . . He was welded into a common personality which was dominated by a single desire. For some moments he could not flee, no more than a little finger can commit a revolution from a hand."

Unlike the pictures he had seen in schoolbooks, in this battle the soldiers didn't seem to be posing for statues. Officers bobbed to and fro and almost stood on their heads as they tried to see the enemy through the smoke. Rifles jerked, and the lids of cartridge boxes flapped unfastened.

One of the soldiers tried to run away. The lieutenant went after him and beat him back into the ranks. His hands were shaking too much for him to reload his gun, so the lieutenant had to help him. Now men were dying. The crying man who had tried to desert was grazed by a bullet. Another grunted and sat down as he was hit in the stomach, a look of reproach in his eyes.

Eventually the firing slowed down, and the men realized that the line had held. Looking around, the youth saw the bodies of the dead in strange positions, arms bent and heads turned in unbelievable ways. He was amazed to observe that fighting was still going on in other places, that the battle just ended was not the only one of the day. And he was also amazed to notice the blue sky and shining sun above. To think that the sun would keep shining through all that!

This chapter is a skillful portrayal of the horror and unreality of war, its strange sounds and smells and movements. Crane describes it in swift, sure strokes, sketching character in a phrase (the "passionate gesture" with which the general rides away) or describing something awful in one sentence ("It seemed that the dead man must have fallen from some great height to get into such positions").

A number of image patterns continue. Going into battle, Jim Conklin knots a red handkerchief around his neck; Henry, in the heat of battle, feels a "red rage." Crane also continues to personify inanimate objects. "The guns squatted in a row like savage chiefs. They argued with abrupt violence. It was a grim pow-pow. Their busy servants ran hither and thither." Crane describes a line of wounded men as "a flow of blood from the torn body of the brigade."

Crane goes on with the imagery of hands and of amputation begun in the previous chapter. The young soldier feels as firmly a part of his regiment as the fingers of a hand, reminding us of Bill's crushed fingers or the lieutenant's wounded hand. "If he had thought the regiment was about to be annihilated perhaps he could have amputated himself from it," Crane tells us, making us think of Bill's refusal to have his hand amputated, or of the description of the lieutenant's hand as a "wounded member." Several hands are hurt in these chapters, but none of them is cut off.

The young soldier is able to fight successfully now because he feels like part of a group. He is a member, a finger on a hand. Because he is not thinking of himself but of the group, he is able to behave courageously.

There have been references to the sun before in the book, but this is the first chapter that closes with the image of the sun shining above the field of battle. Several other chapters will also end this way, and we must be alert for them.

CHAPTER 6

The young soldier relaxed after the battle, picking his cap off the ground, wiping his sweaty face, chatting with the others. Suddenly a cry went up. The Confederate soldiers were attacking again.

But by now the men were exhausted, and they groaned loudly to each other. The youth was near exhaustion: his eyes looked like a tired horse's, his neck was quivering, his arm muscles felt numb, and his knees were weak.

The youth fired a shot. But the soldier next to him turned and ran. Then another young man, who had struck the youth as especially brave, also threw down his gun. Watching them, the young soldier yelled and headed for the rear. He ran wildly, without looking, bumping into trees, sometimes falling down. He thought that the whole regiment was fleeing, and he raced ahead in order to keep as far ahead of the enemy as possible. Eventually the youth came to a battery; the gunners continued to shoot them as if they didn't realize that the army was in retreat. They seemed to him to be fools. Looking to one side, he saw another brigade charging into action to come to their aid. They must be fools, too.

NOTE: Why do you think Henry runs away? Is he a coward? Do you think (as some readers do) that he had no control over what he did, that he was as much an animal as the tired horse he resembled? Or do you think he could have forced himself to stay and fight? Many readers argue over this point.

Later he passed a general and tried to overhear what he was saying to the staff members who surrounded him. He half expected that the general would ask him for advice, and he would give him a piece of his mind for the stupid way he was handling things. Instead, he heard the general order one of his men to send in another regiment to support the center of the line, in danger of breaking. But a moment later, the general jumped up in his saddle. "Yes, by heavens, they've held 'im!" Sending another messenger after the first, the general bounced up and down in his saddle with joy.

The description of the young soldier's flight relies heavily on language Crane has already used. He speaks again of the war god, but in this chapter, "The slaves toiling in the temple of this god began to feel rebellion at his harsh tasks." In the previous chapter the regiment was likened to a body; here, "The sore joints of the regiment creaked. . . . " This language suggests to us that many of the soldiers are ready to flee, preparing us for the youth's action.

In Chapter 4 the youth had been sure that he would flee "if he could have got intelligent control of his legs." In Chapter 2 he had seen the campfires across the river as "the orbs of a row of dragons advancing," and, in Chapter 4, he expected to get a glimpse of "The composite monster which had caused the other troops to flee." In Chapter 6 all of these images come together in his vision of the new Confederate attack as "an onslaught of redoubtable dragons. He became like the man who lost his legs at the approach of the red and green monster. . . . He seemed to shut his eyes and wait to be gobbled." This fantasy is all the more powerful because the youth has previously imagined monsters, and felt that his legs couldn't move.

Once again Crane depicts the machinery as alive. The exploding shells look like "strange war flowers bursting into fierce bloom," an image used before to describe tents in the camp. "The battery was disputing with a distant antagonist," and the gunners "seemed to be patting them on the back and encouraging them with words. The guns, stolid and undaunted, spoke with dogged valor." But while the guns are alive to the young soldier, he sees the gunners as machines: "Methodical idiots! Machine-like fools!" And we remember that he called the Confederate soldiers "machines of steel." Again, there is religious imagery; the decision to run is "a revelation," the general's eyes display "a desire to chant a paean," and there are several references to the war god. The color red appears several times, in a mention of "the red, formidable difficulties of war," in the color of the monster in the legend the young soldier recalls, and in the angry lieutenant's face as he tries to make the youth get back in line. In a way, this chapter, like the previous one, ends with an image of the sun—but this time, the happy general "beamed upon the earth like a sun."

CHAPTER 7

Listening to the cheering, the youth realized that the Union soldiers had won after all. At first he was happy, but then he began to feel annoyed. He tells himself that "he had done a good part in saving himself, who was a little piece of the army. . . . If none of the little pieces were wise enough to save themselves from the flurry of death at such a time, why, then, where would be the army?" The youth begins to think that the other soldiers had been fools who, in their stupidity, had made his intelligent decision look wrong. He began to pity himself, imagining the laughter when he returned to camp.

Trying to get away from the sounds of battle, as well as from his increasingly bad feelings, the youth walked into a forest. But creepers caught on his legs and saplings banged into him. Afraid that all these noises would give away his position, he went deeper into the woods. Now that he could no longer hear the sounds of battle, he felt better. The sun came out, and the insects chirped. "This landscape gave him assurance. A fair field holding life. It was the religion of peace. . . . He conceived Nature to be a woman with a deep aversion to tragedy."

NOTE: When the young soldier is feeling relieved to be in the forest away from the battle, he imagines nature as a woman, peaceful and comforting. This is the way some of the romantic poets and writers of the first half of the nineteenth century wrote about nature. By the end of the century, this view was no longer widely accepted.

In this peaceful place he playfully threw a pine cone at a squirrel, and the animal scurried away. This was the law of nature, the youth told himself; threatened, animals ran. He begins to think that nature forgives him. But in the beautiful forest, he passes through an unpleasant swamp, which could have told him, had he wanted to learn, that nature has more than one face. He saw an animal leap into the black waters and catch a fish—showing another of nature's laws, the triumph of the strong, the survival of the fittest. This is not what the young soldier wants to see.

NOTE: The idea of the survival of the fittest comes from *The Origin of Species* by Charles Darwin. In this book, written at just about the time the action in

The Red Badge of Courage takes place, the English naturalist claimed that in nature, those plants and animals strongest and best adapted to the environment survive, while the weak die off. Darwin was writing about the natural world, but by the 1880s and 1890s other writers were applying his ideas to human society. People like Herbert Spencer and William Graham Sumner wrote books to prove charity was wrong. Poor people should be allowed to die off, while the rich, who were fittest, should survive. And labor unions were wrong, because they made weak people artificially strong, and that ran against the law of nature. People couldn't do very much to change their conditions. This view was called "social Darwinism." The passage about the animal and the fish brings to mind the ideas of both Darwinism and social Darwinism.

Finally he comes to a place like a "chapel," suffused with "a religious half light." Crane is using powerful religious imagery here; this "dark, intricate" place is both the heart of nature and deeply religious. Yet where the chapel's altar should be, the youth sees something else—a man dead and decaying, his face covered with ants. This is really nature's law—not the scampering squirrel, or a woman turning away from tragedy, but death and decay. As the blue uniform turns green, becoming part of the forest, and as ants work their way over the dead soldier's face, his body returns to the earth. Here is a revelation for the youth as compelling as the "revelation" of his need to flee in the previous chapter. When the dead man and the living one stand face to face, the youth must realize that although he can run from a battle, he cannot escape this fate.

CHAPTER 8

The stillness of the forest is shattered by an incredibly loud noise. The youth begins to run in the direction of the battle he just ran away from, because it sounds so big and so important that he thinks he ought to see it.

The youth is beginning to feel ashamed of his flight. No longer does he defend it to himself as correct and intelligent. He begins to look at the experience with some distance: the engagement was probably not even a major battle, although the soldiers thought they were winning the whole war by themselves. Maybe misguided ideas about becoming a hero serve some purpose, because they keep soldiers from deserting.

Once again Crane uses the metaphor of war as a machine. It grinds out corpses, and it mangles men's bodies. And once again Crane uses red to mean warlike, as in the phrases, "crimson roar" and "red cheers." Nature is still holy, but the references to hymns and devotions in the opening of the chapter are somewhat ironic.

Finally he came to a road, where he fell in with a crowd of wounded men. One of them, whose shoe was full of blood, hopped up and down like a schoolboy. Another, who seemed about to die, stared straight ahead. An officer cursed the privates who were kind enough to carry him, and yelled at the crowd to make way. One of the bearers bumped heavily into the dying soldier.

NOTE: This dying man is called the spectral, or ghostly, soldier. Both the man and the word play an important role in the next chapter.

One of the wounded was a man in tatters who was listening with an air of astonishment to a sergeant's tall tales. The sergeant teased him for his lack of sophistication, and the tattered man, embarrassed, shrank back and tried to make friends with the youth. He spoke in a gentle voice, praising the courage of the Union soldiers. "Well, they didn't run t'-day, did they, hey? No, sir! They fit, an' fit, an' fit." Then he asked the youth in a brotherly way, "Where yeh hit, ol' boy?" The youth, horribly ashamed, runs away.

Like the description of the soldiers on the eve of battle several chapters earlier, this scene shows us various types of courage, or lack of it.

CHAPTER 9

The youth found a place to walk where the tattered soldier could not catch up to him. But he still felt guilty about being with this group of wounded soldiers and not being hurt himself. He wished that he had a wound, a "red badge of courage."

NOTE: This is the first place in the book that the title phrase, "the red badge of courage," appears.

He came alongside the ghostly soldier, who walked stiffly, and seemed to be looking for a place to die. Suddenly the youth recognized him, and screamed: "Gawd! Jim Conklin!" It was the tall soldier, his old friend. "Hello, Henry," the dying man replied, and explained that he had worried about the youth during the battle in which he had been wounded.

Henry tried to put his arms around his friend, but the wounded man wanted to walk on his own. As they went along, a terrified look crossed the tall soldier's face, and he told Henry that he was afraid he would fall and be run over by artillery wagons. Henry fervently promised to make certain that that wouldn't happen. The tall soldier continued to beg for reassurance, saying "I've allus been a pretty good feller, ain't I? An' it ain't much t' ask, is it? . . . I'd do it fer you, wouldn't I, Henry?" Henry's only answer is to sob. But as suddenly as he had become afraid, the tall soldier seemed to forget his fears, and brushed Henry aside.

Then the tattered soldier, from whom Henry had run away in shame, came up. He told Henry that a battery was coming through, and that he ought to get the tall soldier off the road to safety. Henry led his friend into the field, when suddenly the dying man began to run. Henry and the tattered man chased him, but Jim kept begging to be left alone. As Henry and the tattered man followed, "They began to have thoughts of a solemn ceremony. There was something ritelike in these movements of the doomed soldier. And there was a resemblance in him to a devotee of a mad religion. . . . They were awed and afraid."

At last, Jim stood still. Henry and the tattered man realized that he had found the right place. Standing up straight, his hands at his sides, "He was waiting with patience for something that he had come to meet. He was at the rendezvous." The dying man's chest began to heave. Again Henry tried to comfort his friend, and again Jim pushed him away. Then Jim began to shake. He fell down, and his "body seemed to bounce a little way from the earth. 'God!' said the tattered soldier." Henry, who had "watched, spellbound, this ceremony at the place of meeting," ran to his friend. Through the flap of his blue jacket, Henry saw that Jim's side looked "as if it had been chewed by wolves." Henry turned toward the battlefield, shaking his fist in fury. Above them, "the red sun was pasted in the sky like a wafer."

This chapter is the symbolic heart of *The Red Badge of Courage*, and the subject of much discussion about the novel's meaning. The religious imagery in this chapter is very powerful indeed. Jim's motions as death approaches seem "like a solemn ceremony," "rite-like," and Jim resembles "a devotee of a mad religion." Some readers identify Jim Conklin with Jesus Christ—their initials are the same. Jim is described as spectral or ghostly, perhaps reminding us of the Holy Ghost. Like Christ, Jim has wounds on his hands and his sides. Some readers even think that the way Jim's body fell as he died—it "seemed to bounce a little way from the earth"—represents the Resurrection.

A strong argument for the identification of Jim with Jesus Christ is Jim's behavior throughout the novel. In the first chapter Jim is the bearer of good tidings (although they do turn out not to be true). The other men in the company seem to recognize his leadership. When Henry is upset about the coming fight, Jim is calm and philosophical; he comforts Henry. He does not boast like the loud soldier, but he is uncomplaining and ready to take whatever comes—including, in this chapter, death. But even in his final moments Jim's concern is for others. He had worried about Henry's safety, he tells his friend when he meets up with him. Begging Henry to help get him out of the road, he cries, "I'd do it fer you."

This chapter's closing line is the most famous in the novel, indeed, one of the most famous in all of American literature. Some people who have written about *The Red Badge of Courage* have called the line contrived and show-offy. Others have tried to show that Crane got the image of the red wafer from Rudyard Kipling's novel, *The Light That Failed*, which was published in 1891. But most critics have been interested in the meaning of the image, not its source. Some think that Crane is describing the way the sun actually looks when viewed through fog or (after a battle) heavy smoke—red and flat, like a wafer. Others believe that the comparison Crane is making is to a wafer of sealing wax, and that that is why he uses the word "pasted." But the most debate has come from the interpretation that the wafer is a communion wafer. People who support this meaning also see Jim Conklin as a Christ figure, whose death redeems Henry.

In deciding what you think about the meaning of the last line, you might remember the last time (in Chapter 5) that an episode closed with an image of the sun. Then the sun streamed down beautifully when the battle appeared to have ended. Is there any relationship between that sun and this red one? (Remember that red in this novel has always been the color of war.) You might compare Henry's reaction to Jim Conklin's death to his reaction to finding the dead soldier in the cathedral of trees in Chapter 7. The first time he confronted a dead man, Henry recoiled in horror. As Jim falls, Henry shakes his hand in the direction of the battlefield and yells, "Hell!" Has this any bearing on the possibility that Jim may represent Jesus Christ?

CHAPTER 10

As this chapter opens, the young soldier and the tattered man are talking about Jim Conklin's death. The tattered man calls him a "reg'lar jim-dandy fer nerve" and wonders "where he got 'is stren'th from?" The youth, too upset to speak, throws himself on the ground. The tattered man reminds him that the tall soldier is dead and no longer needs help, while he "ain't enjoying any great health m'self these days." The young soldier is afraid that he is about to witness another horrible death, but the tattered man assures him that he is not ready to die. He calls the way the tall soldier died "th' funniest thing," and urges the youth to come away—"there ain't no use in our stayin' here an' tryin' t' ask him anything." (The youth, we remember, also wanted to ask a question of the dead man in Chapter 7.)

NOTE: In this chapter, as in Chapter 8 where he first appeared, it's hard to know what to make of the tattered man. The repetition of the phrase "tattered" makes the reader think of a jester or a clown, and sometimes the tattered man seems so simple as to be silly. Indeed, the sergeant in Chapter 8 laughed at him. But the tattered man seems good and innocent, proud of his fellow soldiers, fond of the children he mentions as the reason he isn't going to die.

As they begin to walk along the road, the tattered man tells how he received his wounds. He was fighting, he recalls, and a neighbor from home, Tom Jamison, told him that he had been shot in the head. Until then, he hadn't realized it. Trying to move to the rear, he was hit again, in the arm. The tattered man observes that the young soldier isn't looking well, either. "I bet yeh 've got a worser one than yeh think," he says solicitously. "It might be inside mostly, an' them plays thunder. . . . Yeh might have some queer kind 'a hurt yourself." He keeps asking, "Where is your'n located?"

The youth, feeling terribly ashamed, grumbles, "Oh, don't bother me!" and, looking at the tattered man with hatred, goes off. The tattered man can't believe it. In his confused mind—he seems to be going into a state of shock—the young soldier has become Tom Jamison, and he tells him, "Yeh wanta go trompin' off with a bad hurt. It ain't right—now—Tom Jamison—it ain't. You wanta leave me take keer of yeh, Tom Jamison." Running away, the young soldier sees the tattered man wandering helplessly around the field.

These constant questions about where the wound is located make the young soldier feel terrible, and he turns in anger on the tattered man. Of course, Henry has no wound, and he doesn't want to be found out. But in a way the tattered man is right—Henry's wound is worse than he thinks, and it *is* "inside mostly, an' them plays thunder." Henry's wound is psychological—it is his lack of courage, his shame at deserting his comrades in the heat of battle.

At the chapter's end Henry runs away from this wounded and suffering man who showed so much sympathy for him (and who would not, we realize, have deserted the young soldier in a time of need). The tattered man may be a little ridiculous, but he is kinder than Henry. In the closing lines the tattered soldier represents the society that will find out the young soldier's shame, and he recognizes that he "could not defend himself forever" against it—as if his own fellows, not the Confederates, were the enemy. He wishes he were dead.

CHAPTER 11

This chapter takes place largely in the mind of the young soldier as he tries to come to terms with his desertion and figure out what to do next. It is an impressive psychological portrait of a man at war with himself, struggling with his guilt. The young soldier is still trying to rationalize his flight, and still harbors dreams of glory, but for the most part he recognizes what he has done. As he walks along he alternates between hope and despair, self-justification and self-hatred.

Seeing retreating wagons, teams, and men, Henry comforts himself; if everyone is retreating, he is not so bad. But then he sees a column of infantry marching proudly forward, and he wonders what made them so brave. He recognizes that "He could never be like them." But as his envy grows, he imagines himself a hero "leading lurid charges,"—and fills with plans to start for the front. But then he realizes how hard it would be. He has no rifle. Well, the fields are full of abandoned rifles, he could pick one up. He could never find his regiment. Well, he could fight with any regiment. If he returned, his comrades would realize that he had previously fled. No, they would not see his face in battle. Drained and paralyzed by these conflicts, he realizes that he is hungry, thirsty, and sore.

NOTE: In the jerky, somewhat confused sentences in this chapter, Crane anticipates a technique of writing that was later called "stream of consciousness." The idea is that words and thoughts appear on the page just as they appear in the character's mind—not in nice, neat sentences, but in short, often contradictory phrases.

"A certain mothlike quality within him kept him in the vicinity of the battle." He wanted to know who was winning. Of course, he hoped for a Union victory. At the same time, he realized that a defeat might vindicate him. "A serious prophet upon predicting a flood should be the first man to climb a tree." Besides, defeats are blamed on generals—and usually the wrong ones, at that—not on individual soldiers.

He wanted desperately to be proved right. Otherwise, he feared he would "wear the sore badge of his dishonor through life." "He denounced himself as a villain," and imagined that he was a murderer of the soldiers who were brave enough to fight. Again he wished that he were dead.

But in the end he could not really hope for the defeat of the Union army. He imagined it as a "mighty blue machine" that "would make victories as a contrivance turns out buttons." Realizing that his side would win, he began to envision his return to camp, and wondered how he could explain his absence to the other men. He imagined them laughing and pointing at him. His name would become synonymous with cowardice; he would become "a slang phrase."

Some of the language in this chapter echoes what has gone before. The young soldier's perception of the advancing troops with the "sinuous movement of a serpent" recalls the description of the regiment as a "huge crawling reptile" in Chapter 2. Too, the familiar image of war as a machine reappears here in the reference to the "mighty blue machine" that turns out victories. The image of the young soldier as a moth makes us think of war as a flame, recalling his need for "blaze, blood, and danger" to discover the meaning of courage in Chapter 2. There is some religious language here, too, in the young soldier's likening himself to a "prophet," and his vision of the brave soldiers as "chosen beings." And of course "the sore badge of dishonor" is an ironic contrast to "the red badge of courage."

CHAPTER 12

The column that the young soldier had seen marching so proudly to battle just moments before was now in wild retreat. Surrounded by running soldiers, the youth kept trying to find out what was going on. Finally he clutched one of the soldiers by the arm, and refused to let go. Angry and panicked, the man hit the young soldier fiercely on the head with the butt of his rifle.

The youth saw lightning and heard thunder. He fell down. He got up on his hands and knees, "like a babe trying to walk," and finally stood up. He was afraid to pass out in the middle of the field, because he might be in danger there. He decided to find a safe place; "He went tall soldier fashion." His wounds didn't hurt much, and the dripping blood felt cool and liquid. As he staggered along, scenes of home flashed before the young soldier's eyes. He remembered meals his mother cooked, and thought about the old swimming hole.

Then he heard a "cheery voice" saying, "Yeh seem t' be in a pretty bad way, boy?" The owner of the voice offers to help the young soldier find his regiment. The youth feels much less threatened by this man's questions than he was by those of the tattered man. As they walk, the cheery-voiced man tells the youth about the confusions of the day's battles; everyone was fighting everywhere.

As they walked along, the young soldier thought that the man with the cheery voice possessed "a wand of a magic kind. He threaded the mazes of the tangled forest. . . . Obstacles fell before him. . . ." Finally they found the 304th New York. The man with the cheery voice grasped his hand warmly, and wishing him good luck, walked off. The young soldier realized that

he had never seen the man's face—making the
stranger seem extremely mysterious both to him and
to us.

NOTE: Who is this mysterious man? Is it only the
young soldier who thinks he possesses magical pow-
ers, or are we, too, supposed to see him as somewhat
supernatural?

It is ironic that when the youth finally receives a
wound, a red badge of courage, it is inflicted by the
butt—not the barrel—of a rifle, and by a retreating
soldier in a panic. The young soldier is wounded by a
man very much like himself. Not only had he also
retreated, but he too had been maddened and panicked by another man's questions. Being wounded
turns the young soldier's life around. He falls to the
ground, seeing lightning and hearing thunder, almost
like a revelation. Then he picks himself up, climbing
first to his hands and knees like a baby, and decides to
go "tall soldier fashion." The suggestion in this language is that the wound is like an experience of con-
version. In addition, the image of the young soldier
learning to stand like a baby indicates that he may be
beginning all over again. The phrase "tall soldier fashion" may mean that the young soldier is looking for
the right place to die, as the tall soldier did, but it also
suggests that the young soldier has learned courage
from his dead friend, and now behaves the way Jim
did. (The young soldier carries himself carefully, as
the tall soldier did when he was wounded.)

The man with the cheery voice who befriends him
talks about different kinds of courage. He jokes that
the wounded officer they pass won't boast about his
reputation when they begin sawing off his leg, but he
sympathizes with him too. The story he tells about

Jack, the man in his regiment who was killed, resembles in some way the story of the young soldier and the tattered man, and the young soldier's experience with the soldier who wounded him. Jack, too, would not answer another man's questions, and when he turned angrily to tell the questioner to go to hell, he was killed.

This chapter contains striking descriptions of the chaos of the retreat, as well as some by now familiar imagery: war as "the red animal," the "blood-swollen god," the guns "shaking in black rage," the opposing soldiers as "the dragon," the men in retreat as "terrified buffaloes." (Soldiers fighting are often described as machines, but in trouble or discomfort they become animals.)

CHAPTER 13

As he approached his regiment, the young soldier worried that he was about to face hostility and ridicule. He thought briefly about trying to hide, but he was too hungry and tired. It turned out that he needn't have worried. The sentry—the loud soldier, Wilson—who had given Henry up for dead, was delighted to see him. The young soldier hurriedly concocted a story about where he had been. He said that he'd been separated from the regiment and had been fighting on the right, where he had been shot in the head.

Wilson called the corporal, Simpson, to take care of Henry. Simpson examined his head in the firelight, running his fingers through Henry's hair until "his fingers came in contact with the splashed blood and the rare wound." He concluded that Henry had been grazed by a cannonball but not seriously hurt. The wound was no longer bleeding, he found, and "It's raised a queer lump jest as if some feller had lammed yeh on th' head with a club." Simpson doesn't know how right he is!

When Simpson leaves him, promising to send Wilson over, Henry looks around. Soldiers are scattered all over, "lying deathlike in slumber." Across the fire, the young soldier notices an officer asleep with his back against a tree. The overhanging trees make the spot appear like a "low-arched hall," and through them Henry can see stars.

The description of the regiment's camp echoes the forest depicted in Chapter 7. There, hiding from his shame, the young soldier entered a cathedral-like space streaming with sunlight. In the forest cathedral he had seen the decaying soldier propped up against a tree. Here the description is similar, but the mood is very different. The forest where the regiment is camped resembles a "low-arched hall," and the light comes from the stars. Staring across at the young soldier is another man propped up against a tree, but he is only sleeping. And the other soldiers strewn around the fire, "lying deathlike," are similarly asleep. Does this suggest that the young soldier encountered horror when he was running away, but that when he returns to his responsibilities the scene is drained of horror?

The young soldier is welcomed warmly back into the fellowship of the regiment; Wilson treats him extremely kindly. (More kindly, in fact, than is consistent with his character as we have seen it in earlier chapters.) But what does it mean that the young soldier, as he falls asleep, is "like his comrades"? He is like them because he is sleeping wrapped in a blanket, but does Crane mean that he is now one of them again, as brave as they are? After all, we know, even if

Wilson and Simpson don't, how Henry was separated from the regiment, and how he was wounded. Does that no longer matter? Or is Crane, in this sentence, being ironic?

CHAPTER 14

This chapter shows how much Wilson has changed and grown up. Wilson helped the young soldier to dress his wound and get some breakfast. Wilson was a clumsy nurse, and when the youth snapped at him, he apologized quietly. An enormous change seemed to have come over Wilson, the young soldier reflected. "He was no more a loud young soldier. . . . He showed a quiet belief in his purposes and his abilities. . . . The youth wondered where had been born these new eyes. . . ." The young soldier points out the change to Wilson, who replies, "I believe I was a pretty big fool in those days." This loud young soldier, so full of himself, has become calm, self-assured, and gentle. His growth parallels that of the young soldier.

NOTE: It seems as if Wilson is almost a new person. We haven't seen what happened to him in the previous day's battle, because we were following Henry. What do you think might have happened to change him so? Does it seem possible to you that someone would become so different after only one day of fighting?

The two talk quietly about the previous day's fighting, and the young soldier tells Wilson about Jim Conklin's death. As the young soldier describes what he saw, we realize that he has seen battle, even if he didn't quite participate in it. Still, he talks to Wilson as if he really had seen fighting—"Why, lord, man, you didn't see nothing of the fight." That isn't precisely true. The chapter's ending is curious. Wilson tells the young soldier that many other men disappeared "Jest like you done." With the young soldier, we are inclined to ask, "So?" Does this mean that some really were separated from the regiment by accident, or that other men deserted and then returned to the regiment?

CHAPTER 15

This chapter is interesting for its portrayal of the change in the young soldier's character. Now that both he and his secret are safe, he begins to take pride in the events of the previous day, seeing himself as brave and manly. Some soldiers ran away in terror; he fled with dignity. He realizes that much of what happens in battle is by chance, and that you can get away with a lot. He remembers that Wilson, too, had been afraid on the eve of the first battle, and handing back his friend's letters he feels a little superior to him. The image of a flower appears again, but now it is neither tents nor shells that flower, but the young soldier's confidence. Most of the familiar imagery in this chapter is likewise ironic. Henry's legs are "self-confident," he is "chosen of the gods," he has faced "dragons." In earlier chapters these images had real power. Now Crane employs the kind of high-flown language he often uses when he is making fun of his characters' pretensions. The young soldier realizes that he will be able to go home with a fine fund of war stories. Is Crane being ironic here? Or has the young soldier really learned a kind of courage? We'll find out in the next chapters.

CHAPTER 16

The next day the young soldier's regiment relieves troops that have been fighting in the trenches. Kept there for a while, some of the soldiers begin to criticize their leaders' hesitation. The young soldier, to his amazement, hears himself complaining that everything is the general's fault—"Don't we do all that men can?" Another soldier asks him whether he thinks he fought the whole battle yesterday. Instantly the young soldier is terrified: the question "pierced" him, and his legs "quaked," almost as if he were in battle again. But the other man didn't know the truth. The youth relaxed, but in response "He suddenly became a modest person."

NOTE: The word *pierced* suggests that the other soldier's question is almost like a bullet, reminding us of the end of Chapter 10 where the young soldier begins to feel that the scorn of his comrades, not the Confederate soldiers, is the real enemy. And it's interesting that his legs are quaking now, because the feeling of his legs is always an indication of how brave or frightened the young soldier feels.

This chapter, too, reveals the young soldier's developing character. Before the first battle he had been preoccupied with the question of whether he would run from fire (although he also complained to Jim Conklin about the commanders). This time he boasts about the regiment's bravery, and is critical of the generals, even though he knows exactly how brave he himself had been. Shame and fear shut him up for awhile, but soon he begins to grouse again. The young soldier is still struggling with himself.

CHAPTER 17

In this chapter the young soldier who has pre-
tended to be a hero really becomes one. But, interest-
ingly enough, Crane describes his heroism almost
entirely in terms of animals. The young soldier, in his
anger at the enemy, feels like a "kitten," and thinks he
will develop teeth and claws. He yells back at Wilson
with "a curlike snarl," and as he looks around him,
"the fighters resembled animals tossed for a death
struggle into a dark pit." He chases after the retreating
enemy like a "dog," and at the end of the battle the
lieutenant calls him a "wild cat." Finally, as he thinks
about the battle, he realizes that he has fought like a
"beast." One meaning of these images seems to be
that the young soldier has fought like a hero through
animal instinct; another might be that real heroism in
warfare does not resemble the young soldier's pretty
dreams, but is in fact bestial. The religious imagery in
this chapter backs up this idea. The youth has been a
"barbarian," and has "fought like a pagan who
defends his religion." The youth's heroism has a psychological explanation as well: his exhaustion has
turned to a blind fury at the enemy, and he has been
so angry he could barely think.

At the end of this chapter the sun again appears. As
before, it reflects the young soldier's mood. No longer
a red wafer, this sun is "bright and gay," and the sky
is "blue, enameled."

CHAPTER 18

Several incidents in this chapter remind us of
events that have occurred elsewhere in the novel. The
death of Jimmie Rogers, thrashing about in the grass,

reminds us of the similar death of Jim Conklin, although Jim did not scream the way Jimmie does.

NOTE: The descriptions of the deaths of Jim Conklin and Jimmie Rogers do not seem all that horrible to us. We see worse every time we go to the movies or watch the news on TV. But death had never before been described this realistically in an American novel. Many readers at the time were shocked and disturbed by passages like this.

The "jangling general" who almost runs over a wounded man resembles the way the men who were carrying the wounded officer bumped into the dying Jim Conklin. The young soldier has overheard officers twice before. Once he heard the "gigantic" colonel who was silhouetted against the sky in Chapter 2 talk with an aide about cigars. Then during his flight in Chapter 6 he encountered another general, this one surrounded by a "jingling staff." He thought that he would tell that general what was really going on. He had heard him send in reinforcements, and express delight that the center had held while he bounced around in his saddle.

The encounter with the general in this chapter is slightly different. This time the youth's vision is somewhat more realistic. And what he hears is even more disillusioning than the exchange about the cigars. He realizes that the officers think very little of the 304th; the men have been proud of the way they'd been fighting, but the officer calls them "mule drivers" and says that he can easily spare them. Neither the officer nor the general seems to care that many men of the 304th will die in the coming assault. Fleming's thought that "New eyes were given to him. And the most startling thing was to learn suddenly that he was very insignificant" sounds identical to his meditation in Chapter 14 on the way battle had changed his friend Wilson. "The youth wondered where had been born these new eyes. . . . Apparently, the other had now climbed a peak of wisdom from which he could perceive himself as a very wee thing." The unimportance of the individual appears to be an important lesson of war, contrary to romantic daydreams where individual heroes triumph. The young soldier had hoped to hear "some great inner historical things." Perhaps he really did.

NOTE: The theme of understanding things better and seeing more clearly is pursued in several ways. Because Henry and Wilson leave the fighting in which they have up until now been engaged, they are able to see the layout of the whole battle. They notice a road, a battery of guns, and a house whose windows glowed "a deep murder red."

CHAPTER 19

This chapter repeats the theme of courage as bestial instinct. The young soldier is described running "as if pursued for a murder," his eyes have "a lurid glare," his features are "red and inflamed," and he looked "insane." Even the red badge of courage makes the young soldier look a little crazy. Henry is in the advance of his regiment, but "unconsciously." The soldiers rush in a "frenzy," "moblike and barbaric," with "mad enthusiasm," in a "delirium." Only when this feeling subsides do they become men again.

The narrator makes a number of statements in this chapter, most of them about this frenzied fighting. Previously the narrative voice has described only characters—usually a bit ironically—not actions. But now the narrator says that this enthusiasm and delirium is a "sublime absence of selfishness," presumably one of the definitions of courage. Later the narrator adds that the men's "lack of a certain feeling of responsibility for being there" was "the dominant animal failing." When the young soldier charges forward again, he runs "like a madman," his mouth dripping saliva.

NOTE: The major battles of the Civil War, such as Chancellorsville, consisted of many small skirmishes like the ones Henry participated in. As we see in these chapters, the blue soldiers and the gray soldiers engage, retreat, rest, and clash again. Eventually one group or the other wins, and the battle is over.

Even during World War II that was what war was like. But in our day war has become very different. The opposing sides don't always wear uniforms; in fact, the enemy may be civilians, not soldiers. There may not be fixed battles where a line of soldiers charges, but the constant sniping of guerillas instead. And it isn't always clear when an engagement is over, or who has won or lost.

What would it mean to be courageous in a modern war? Do you think that Stephen Crane's definition of courage—not thinking of yourself and acting on instinct—makes any sense for the kinds of wars we have today?

The young soldier's rush to rescue the falling flag is, of course, a courageous act. Yet his feeling of love for the flag, and his personification of it as "a goddess . . . a woman, red and white, hating and loving," seems to be the kind of romantic dream that he has begun to move beyond. Still, the details of the dying soldier's death grip on the flagpole, and his hand on Wilson's shoulder, provide a realistic, even macabre finish to this romantic episode.

CHAPTER 20

In this part of the battle the young soldier acts extremely bravely, trying to halt the retreat by encouraging the men, and then by raising the flag high.

The images are all somewhat familiar. The regiment is likened to a machine running down, and also to an animal, "vicious" and "wolflike." It is also compared to a broom, an image that was used in Chapter 18 when the officer "spoke of the regiment as if he referred to a broom. Some part of the woods needed sweeping, perhaps, and he merely indicated a broom in a tone properly indifferent to its fate." Now the unimportant broom has become terribly aggressive as the young soldier thinks to himself "that if the enemy was about to swallow the regimental broom as a large prisoner, it could at least have the consolation of going down with bristles forward." The image of the young lieutenant as a baby is also familiar. In Chapter 19, for example, there is reference to his "infantile features" and the "soft and childlike curve" of his lips.

CHAPTER 21

When the enemy troops pulled back, the 304th regiment returned to its own lines. But to their surprise, the veterans who were waiting there made fun of

them. "Goin' home now, boys?" The youth was furious, and some of the men challenged the veterans to
fights, but most of them hung their heads. As the
youth looked around, he realized that they had not in
fact covered much ground, and that the engagement
had not lasted very long. He was annoyed at his comrades, although he took pleasure in the way he had
conducted himself.

The general who had called them mule drivers galloped up, and began to yell at Colonel MacChesnay.
"If your men had gone a hundred feet farther you
would have made a great charge, but as it is—what a
lot of mud diggers you've got anyway!" The colonel
seemed ready to argue with him, but instead he
shrugged his shoulders and said that they had fought
as well as they could. The lieutenant insisted to the
colonel that the boys had put up a good fight, but the
colonel brushed him away.

Fleming and Wilson were talking together when
another soldier came up to tell them that Lieutenant
Hasbrouck had praised them both to the colonel. The
colonel had asked who carried the flag, and the lieutenant had told him "That's Flemin', an' he's a jim-
hickey." He added that Wilson had headed the
charge the whole time. "They deserve t' be major generals," the colonel said. The two delighted friends
thought that both the colonel and the lieutenant were
terrific.

CHAPTER 22

This chapter is a portrait of two armies at war. As
the flag bearer, the youth observed the next phase of
the battle almost as a spectator. He saw two regiments
slugging it out together as if they were playing a
game; another regiment marched proudly into the

woods, made an enormous racket, and marched just as proudly out. On the left there was "a long row of guns, gruff and maddened, denouncing the enemy"; their "red discharges" formed a "crimson flare." The gray soldiers drew back, and the blue ones cheered. For a minute all was quiet and "churchlike."

Suddenly the noise began again, "the whirring and thumping of gigantic machinery." The men surged at each other. The youth saw some gray soldiers "go in houndlike leaps" toward the blue ones; they "went away with a vast mouthful of prisoners." Then a "blue wave" dashed against a "gray obstruction," while the flags flew like "crimson foam." The regiment occasionally let forth "barbaric cries," and the lieutenant kept inventing new oaths.

NOTE: This is the language we have come to recognize. The guns speak ("denouncing"), the brave soldiers are like animals ("houndlike") or savages ("barbaric cries"). Religious imagery appears too; the occasional silence is "churchlike." You can almost imagine what this would look like as a painting—the blue waves dashing against gray rocks, with crimson foam splashing. In this comparison of the battle to a sea, Crane suggests that war is a force of nature.

The enemy soldiers took shelter behind a fence, and the regiment battered against it. Many of them remembering that the general had called them mud diggers tried especially hard to get rid of the Confederates. The youth imagined his dead body in the middle of the field as proof to the general that the regiment had fought well. The lieutenant appeared to be on "his last box of oaths," and Wilson looked frazzled and dirty. The regiment seemed to be foundering.

CHAPTER 23

In this chapter the youth, his friend, and the regiment all behave extremely bravely. For all of them the heroic activity is automatic ("there was no obvious questioning, nor figurings, nor diagrams"). All display the frenzy, enthusiasm, and unselfishness praised by the narrator in Chapter 19. There is a suggestion of barbarism in the youth's feeling "like a savage, religion-mad" (we remember that in Chapter 17 he had fought "like a pagan who defends his religion") and in his vision of the Confederate flag as a "treasure of mythology." He feels a "wild battle madness." The description of the regiment's final thrust at the Confederate soldiers, "racing as if to achieve a sudden success before an exhilarating fluid should leave them," has an almost sexual suggestion.

This is also a chapter of vivid color. The men "in dusty and tattered blue" rush "over a green sward and under a sapphire sky," while the youth "kept the bright colors to the front." The Confederate flag has a "red brilliancy."

The regiment takes four prisoners. One nursed a wounded foot, and swore at the blue soldiers as if someone had stepped on his foot accidentally. Another, a young boy, seemed composed, and talked cheerfully with his captors. The third looked sad and said no more than "Ah, go t' hell!" The fourth was silent, and seemed to be overwhelmed by shame. The attitudes of these Confederate prisoners greatly resemble those of the Union soldiers, a closing irony.

NOTE: We don't meet many Confederate soldiers in *The Red Badge of Courage*, but whenever we do they seem to be very much like Henry and his bud-

dies. Can you think of any time in the novel when any
of the soldiers have talked or thought about why
they're fighting, or what the war is about? What does
this say about Crane's view of wars in general and the
Civil War in particular?

CHAPTER 24

As the regiment, having won its skirmish, with-
draws, Henry Fleming evaluates his experiences in
battle and recognizes that he has achieved "a quiet
manhood." Religious imagery is at work here. At first
the young soldier recalls his heroism, and "saw that
he was good"—an echo of God's assessment of cre-
ation in Genesis 1:31 ("And God saw **every** thing that
he had made, and, behold, it was **very** good"). But
eventually the youth rejects his "earlier gospels." So
doing, he is able to put the shame of his desertion and
the "sin" of his abandonment of the tattered soldier
behind him. Flowers appear again, in the line "scars
faded as flowers"; and we see the purple and gold of
Henry's vanity and the "red of blood and black of
passion." Henry rids himself of the "red sickness of
battle."

Throughout *The Red Badge of Courage* the young soldier has tried to understand death. In Chapter 3 he
seemed to want to ask a question of the dead soldier
in the yellow suit. In Chapter 7 he exchanged a long
look with the dead soldier in the forest. And in Chapter 10 the tattered man tells him that the dead Jim
Conklin isn't going to tell him anything. But by the
battle's end Henry understands what death means.
"He had been to touch the great death, and found
that, after all, it was but the great death."

As the young soldier takes stock of himself, conversation swirls around him. Someone praises the young lieutenant: "Hasbrouck? He's th' best off'cer in this here reg'ment." Bill Smithers—whose hand was stepped on back in Chapter 2 but who wouldn't let the doctor amputate his fingers—is quoted as saying that life in the hospital, which is shelled every night, is much more dangerous than fighting. As he has all along, Smithers is malingering, acting like a coward. Henry had been afraid that the other soldiers would laugh at him if they found out the story of his flight. But although they laugh at Smithers, it's with affection. Smithers laughs at himself; his cowardice is not a terrible shame.

The nature imagery with which the chapter ends supports the message of redemption carried by the religious imagery. The young soldier can't wait to see fresh meadows and cool brooks (although some readers point out that the peacefulness of nature was decisively rejected in Chapter 8). At the close of the book the sun, ever the mirror of Henry's feelings, breaks through the heavy clouds.

A STEP BEYOND

Tests and Answers

TESTS

Test 1

1. The specific Civil War battle that is recounted _____
in the novel is
A. the Battle of Bull Run
B. the Battle of Gettysburg
C. not identified

2. Stephen Crane refrains from naming many of _____
his characters in order to
A. stimulate the reader's creativity
B. lend universality to his work
C. maintain the unpredictability of the novel

3. Henry's mother had _____
A. discouraged him from enlisting
B. encouraged him to serve his country with
pride
C. refrained from stating an opinion about
enlistment

4. In giving advice, Henry's mother told him _____
I. never to shirk his duty
II. to avoid liquor
III. not to curse
A. I and II only
B. II and III only
C. I, II, and III

5. When the veterans told stories of war, _____
Henry

A. discounted their boasting
B. was boggle-eyed with excitement
C. tried to act blasé and pay no attention

6. When Henry heard that his regiment would   ____
be going into combat, he asked
A. "Think any of the boys 'll run?"
B. "Do they outnumber us?"
C. "Do I have time to write to my Mom?"

7. Some critics suggest there is religious   ____
symbolism in
A. Henry's self-pity
B. the lieutenant's reference to the Ten
Commandments
C. Jim Conklin's name and his wounds

8. When Henry said that he was "about to be   ____
measured," he was referring to the
A. issuance of Army uniforms
B. testing of his bravery
C. questioning of his loyalty to the Union

9. After the first bloody battle, Henry was   ____
A. driven to despair
B. bleeding, exhausted, and depressed
C. somewhat pleased with himself

10. Prior to the first battle, Henry was   ____
A. plagued by self-doubt
B. convinced that he might be a medal
winner
C. fatalistic about his ability to survive

11. What is the meaning of the title, *The Red Badge of Courage*?

12. What is the meaning of courage in this book?

13. How does the character of the young soldier change in
the course of the novel?

14. What is the role of nature in *The Red Badge of Courage?*

15. At the close of *The Red Badge of Courage,* the young soldier tells himself that "he was a man." Is he right? Why or why not?

Test 2

1. When Henry deserted the battle and fled, his _____ fears
    A. diminished
    B. were magnified
    C. remained as potent as they had been

2. As Henry marched along with the wounded _____ soldiers, he
    A. envied them
    B. felt pity for them
    C. felt pride in being associated with them

3. The truly amazing thing about Jim Conklin _____ was
    A. the manner of his death
    B. his Southern drawl, considering that he came from Pennsylvania
    C. his ability to win the love of his enemies

4. Henry distinguished himself from others who _____ had deserted the battle, thinking that
    A. "he had fled with discretion and dignity"
    B. "they would never be able to hold up their heads again"
    C. "there was nothing so hideous as possessing a faint heart"

5. When Wilson had expected to die, he _____
    A. knelt in the woods to offer a tearful prayer
    B. gave Henry a packet of letters for safekeeping

    C. asked the others to excuse his show of
       fear

6. Henry overheard one of the generals referring   _____
   to his men in a derogatory fashion as
   A. mule drivers
   B. senseless sheep
   C. vacant-eyed camels

7. Henry received his "battle wound" from   _____
   A. an officer who labeled him a deserter
   B. a retreating infantryman from his own
      army
   C. a stray bullet

8. Henry and Wilson won praise for   _____
   A. aiding the wounded while under fire
   B. infiltrating the enemy's lines
   C. bravery in carrying the flag

9. It is reasonable to describe *The Red Badge of*   _____
   Courage as
   A. an exultation of regionalism
   B. a voyage of self-discovery
   C. an analysis of the militaristic spirit

10. "And the youth saw that ever after it would be   _____
   easier to live in his friend's neighborhood" is a
   reference to
   A. Jim Conklin's willingness to sacrifice
      himself
   B. the considerable change in Wilson's
      behavior
   C. the tattered man's genuine attempt to
      comfort Henry Fleming

11. What role does the loud soldier play in the novel?

12. Is *The Red Badge of Courage* a Christian allegory of
   redemption? Why or why not?

13. Is *The Red Badge of Courage* a naturalistic novel?

14. Is *The Red Badge of Courage* a Civil War novel? Or is it about any war, or even any battle with yourself?

15. How would *The Red Badge of Courage* be different if Stephen Crane had written it today? Could you write a novel like *The Red Badge of Courage* about the Vietnam War, for example, or some other modern war?

ANSWERS

Test 1

1. C   **2.** B   **3.** A   **4.** C   **5.** A   **6.** A
7. C   **8.** B   **9.** C   **10.** A

    11. The young soldier, Henry Fleming, uses the phrase, "the red badge of courage," in Chapter 8. By it he means a wound. He wishes he had one so that he would look like, and be, a real soldier. He thinks that being wounded in battle proves that you are courageous.

But when Henry is actually wounded in Chapter 12 it is by accident. He is hit on the head by a Union soldier in panic-stricken retreat. Neither Henry nor the soldier who wounds him has been courageous. But Henry's bloody head makes the other soldiers accept him when he returns to camp in Chapter 13. They believe that he has been fighting with another regiment, even though the lump on his head looks like just what it is. And even Henry begins to pretend to himself that he has been courageous after all.

Ironically, when Henry shows real courage in battle, in Chapters 17–23, he is not wounded. The real badge of courage is inside, and the proof of courage is deeds.

The title tells us that this book is about the difference between what courage looks like and what it really is. (See "Themes.")

12.   To understand the meaning of courage in this book, look at the behavior of characters who are courageous. One of these is Jim Conklin, the tall soldier. Before the battle in Chapter 3 he is not afraid that he will run away, and he expects to do what the rest of the regiment does. He follows orders and remains calm. (Henry, in contrast, is very frightened.) In Chapter 9 Jim faces death matter-of-factly. He does not complain about his wounds. Even though he is in pain, he is worried about Henry's safety.

When Henry becomes courageous during the second day's battle (in Chapters 17, 19, and 23) he does not think about himself or about danger. He does what has to be done. He is in a frenzy, like an animal or a savage. During the final charge in Chapter 23 the whole regiment behaves this way.

The next thing to look for is what the narrator says about courage. Although the narrator rarely makes comments, he does so in Chapter 17 when he says that courage is "a temporary but sublime absence of selfishness." (See "Themes.")

13.   Look at the way the young soldier behaves from chapter to chapter. When he joins the army in Chapter 1 he is full of romantic dreams and enjoys playing soldier. In Chapter 2 he is gripped by the fear that he will run away from the battle. After he does so, his thoughts are dominated by rationalizations (Chapters 6 and 7). In Chapters 8–12 Henry's fear turns to shame, and the shame leads him to abandon the tattered soldier. After he returns to his regiment, relief makes him overconfident and obnoxious (Chapter 15). But in the end he fights courageously (Chapters 17, 19, 20, and 23). As the novel comes to a close, he can realistically evaluate his behavior, recognizing both the good and the bad. So Henry changes from being fearful and romantic to understanding what war is, and having confidence in his abilities. He becomes neither over- nor underconfident. He learns to face who he is honestly. And by the end of the book he has learned a concern for his fellows that he did not have in the beginning.

Or you might believe that the young soldier's character does not change during the course of the book. You might look for behavior that proves that he doesn't know himself very well, and that his dreams of peace are as romantic as his early dreams of war. (See ''The Characters.'')

14. Look for descriptions of nature in the novel. They are frequent. Generally, nature is described as being indifferent to war and the affairs of men. The beauty of nature contrasts with the horrors of war. (Notice, for example, the description of the sun at the end of Chapter 5.)

After the young soldier has run from the first battle, he goes into the woods, thinking that the sight of trees will make him feel better. When he throws a pine cone at a squirrel and the animal scampers off, he thinks that nature agrees with him, and that the law of nature is to protect yourself. He does not notice an animal diving into a swamp and coming up with a fish in its teeth. The real law of nature is eat or be eaten. In the heart of the forest Henry comes face to face with a dead soldier whose body is decayed and returning to the forest. That, too, is the law of nature.

But although Crane seems to be saying that nature doesn't care about people, Henry continues to feel that nature mirrors his moods. Trying to get out of the forest in Chapter 8, he thinks the brambles hold him back. And the way the sun looks in the sky usually tells us how Henry is feeling. It is blood red in Chapter 9 after Jim dies; gay and bright after Henry's successful fighting in Chapter 17; and it breaks through the clouds when he comes to terms with himself at the end of Chapter 24.

15. Think about what makes a person mature or manly. Then think about the way Henry's character has changed during the course of the novel. (See ''The Characters'' and the answer to Question 3.) If you agree with Henry, you would argue that he has become a man because: he has given up his dreams of glory; learned that he is part of a whole; fought with real courage; looked upon the great death; and stopped seeing himself as either a hero or a coward, but as somebody who has a little of both in him.

If you disagree with Henry, you would say that he has not really become a man because: his feelings about the flag (Chapter 19) are as silly and romantic as anything he thought before he joined the army; he tends to present himself as surer of things than he really is (as in Chapter 15); his performance during the second battle comes from animal instinct, not from his individual character; and his view of nature in Chapter 24 denies his experience in the forest in Chapter 7.

Test 2

1. B   **2.** A   **3.** A   **4.** A   **5.** B   **6.** A
7. B   **8.** C   **9.** B   **10.** B

11.   Read the section on "The Characters" and look at the places in the novel where the loud soldier appears, for examples of his behavior.

The loud soldier helps us to evaluate Henry's behavior by providing us with an example of another young soldier. At first the loud soldier doesn't seem to be frightened by the approaching battle (Chapters 1 and 2). But just before the fighting begins we see that he thinks he's going to die (Chapter 3). This shows us that like the young soldier, he is really worried, and it lets us know that Henry is typical of other young men.

The loud soldier is apparently changed by battle, because when we meet him again in Chapter 13 he is kind and calm. In Chapter 14 Henry notices that the loud soldier (who is now called "the friend") has come to a better understanding

of his importance in the world. The loud soldier's maturation prepares us for a similar change in Henry. When the
loud soldier fights courageously at Henry's side in the closing chapters of the book, it shows us, again, that Henry is
not so unusual.

12.   Read the section on "The Critics," the discussion of
Jim Conklin in "The Characters," and look closely at the
analysis of Chapter 9 in "The Story."

Some readers have seen *The Red Badge of Courage* as a
story about Christian redemption. They see the red sun
pasted in the sky like a wafer at the end of Chapter 9 as a
symbol of the communion wafer, and Jim Conklin, whose
initials are J.C., as a symbol of Jesus Christ. They say that
Jim's death redeems Henry's sin in running away and sets
him on the path to salvation.

To argue in favor of this position, use the details provided
in the discussion of Chapter 9. These include Jim's character, his initials, his wounds, and the description of his death
as "rite-like."

To argue against, you could say that not all of the details
about Jim fit. Does his body bouncing a little way off the
ground as he dies really mean the resurrection? Also, Jim is
described as looking like "a devotee of a mad religion"—
which couldn't be Christianity. In addition, courage is
described as being animal-like or pagan, not Christian. So as
Henry becomes courageous, he is becoming less Christian,
not more. You could also argue that the sun really looks red
through smoke, and that the sun in Chapter 9, like the suns
in Chapters 5, 17, and 24, only echoes Henry's mood, which
in this case is awful. Finally, if you read the section on "The
Author and His Times," you will see that Stephen Crane
was the son, grandson, and nephew of Methodist clergy-
men. What would a Methodist have to do with communion
wafers?

13.   Naturalism is a belief that people are powerless and that their lives are controlled by heredity and/or environment (including the economy). Naturalists see man as having an animal nature. They tend to be amoral (without morality) unsentimental, frank, and objective.

Does *The Red Badge of Courage* fit any of these descriptions? To some extent it does. Crane frequently describes war as an animal or a machine. Individual soldiers are also described as animals and machines; they lose their identity in the group. Heroic behavior is shown to be instinctive (and animal at that). Henry Fleming doesn't have much choice in what happens to him. He thinks of the regiment as a "moving box" (Chapter 2) that traps him. Nature is shown to be indifferent to what happens to men. Some of the descriptions of death and battle are quite graphic and upsetting.

But *The Red Badge of Courage* is not a totally naturalistic novel. Henry is shown as having some choice (in going back to the regiment, for example). The example of Bill Smithers (see "The Characters") shows that he could have gone to the hospital. Some descriptions are frank, but others are not; the soldiers do not use profanity. And the end of the book tends to be somewhat hopeful, which most naturalistic novels are not.

14.   *The Red Badge of Courage* takes place during the Battle of Chancellorsville in May 1863, but Crane gives very little detail about the Civil War. In fact, he never tells us straight out the name of the battle Henry is fighting in. We can figure it out only by putting some clues (like the name of the river in Chapter 16) together. He doesn't tell us the names of the sides, only the colors of their uniforms. He doesn't tell us when the action is taking place. And he doesn't even tell us where Henry is from, although again we can figure it out from hints.

By calling his characters "the young soldier," "the tall

soldier," "the loud soldier," "the tattered man," and so on, Crane seems to suggest that they are types, not individuals. This is a story about human behavior, not about these particular people. So you cannot really call *The Red Badge of Courage* a Civil War novel.

You could even say that *The Red Badge of Courage* isn't really about war at all. The important thing that happens in this book is that Henry works his way through romantic dreams, fear, self-delusion, and shame to become genuinely brave and to reach a realistic view of himself and his place in the world. You could say that this is what it means to grow up, and that other people growing up go through the same stages, whether or not they are soldiers. Someone could grow up in the course of a crisis or an exciting adventure, for example.

15.   If you believe that courage is still possible in modern wars, you could say that you could write a novel like *The Red Badge of Courage* about the Vietnam War. It would have to be about a young soldier growing up in the course of the war, and learning what it means to be brave. (It might mean something different than it did to Henry.) If you don't believe that courage exists in modern war, you would have to answer no. You might say that you could write a novel about the Vietnam War, but it would be much more bitter and cynical than *The Red Badge of Courage*. Or the hero might not be a soldier, but a doctor or a civilian injured.

Term Paper Ideas

1.   Henry Fleming: hero or coward?

2.   Does Henry Fleming have a will of his own?

3.   Henry Fleming's romantic dreams.

4.   Does Henry Fleming really change?

5. Is Henry Fleming a typical soldier or a typical human being?

6. The role of other characters (Mrs. Fleming, Jim Conklin, Bill Smithers, Lieutenant Hasbrouck, and the tattered man) in *The Red Badge of Courage*.

7. What is courage?

8. The courageous woman. Can a woman show courage, in Stephen Crane's terms, or is it reserved for men? Does Mrs. Fleming show courage?

9. War as a test of character in *The Red Badge of Courage*.

10. Fantasies and realities of war in *The Red Badge of Courage*.

11. Read an account in a history book of the Battle of Chancellorsville and compare it to *The Red Badge of Courage*.

12. Imagery (i.e., animal, mechanical, religious, sun, color) in *The Red Badge of Courage*.

13. Divide the chapters of *The Red Badge of Courage* into four quarters that make sense to you and defend the pattern you come up with.

14. How are the first and last chapters different from the others?

15. What is the effect of Crane's use of short paragraphs?

16. *The Red Badge of Courage* as a naturalistic or realistic novel.

17. *The Red Badge of Courge* as a religious allegory.

18. The psychological realism of *The Red Badge of Courage*.

19. Read some of Stephen Crane's newspaper reporting and compare its style to *The Red Badge of Courage*.

20. Read some poems by Stephen Crane, especially the famous "War Is Kind." How do Crane's poetic styles and subjects compare with those of *The Red Badge of Courage*?

Further Reading
CRITICAL WORKS

Bassan, Maurice. *Stephen Crane: A Collection of Critical Essays.* New York, 1967.

Bergon, Frank. *Stephen Crane's Artistry.* New York, 1975.

Berryman, John. *Stephen Crane.* New York, 1950.

Cady, Edwin. *Stephen Crane.* New York, 1980.

Gullason, Thomas. *Stephen Crane's Career: Perspectives and Evaluations.* New York, 1972.

Katz, Joseph, ed. *Stephen Crane in Transition: Centenary Essays.* New York, 1972.

Nagel, James. *Stephen Crane and Literary Impressionism.* New York, 1980.

Stallman, Robert. *Stephen Crane: A Biography.* New York, 1968.

Walcutt, Charles C. *American Literary Naturalism: A Divided Stream.* Minneapolis, 1956, pp. 66–82.

Weatherford, Richard, ed. *Stephen Crane: The Critical Heritage.* New York, 1973.

AUTHOR'S OTHER WORKS

Novels

Maggie: A Girl of the Streets (1893, 1896). The story of how circumstances force Maggie Johnson to become a prostitute. One of the first naturalistic novels, and one of the first set in an urban slum.

George's Mother (1896). Another novel set in a slum.
The Monster (1899). A hideously injured man is ostracized by his smalltown neighbors.

Short Stories

"An Experiment in Misery" (1894). A young man decides to see what it's like to be down and out.

"The Men in the Storm" (1894). A crowd of poor men wait outside a soup kitchen during a snowstorm.

"A Mystery of Heroism" (1895). A war story.

"The Veteran" (1896). The story of Henry Fleming's death.

"The Open Boat" (1897). Crane's most famous story.

"The Bride Comes to Yellow Sky" (1898). The story of a fight that didn't take place, set in Texas.

"The Blue Hotel" (1898). A stranger is killed when a fight breaks out over a game of cards.

"An Episode of War" (1899). A soldier is injured.

"The Upturned Face" (1900). Two soldiers bury their comrade.

Thomas Gullason, ed. *The Complete Short Stories of Stephen Crane.* Garden City, N.Y., 1963.

The Critics

Henry's regeneration is brought about by the death of Jim Conklin . . . but there are unmistakable hints . . . that he is intended to represent Jesus Christ. . . . Crane intended to suggest here the sacrificial death celebrated in communion . . . the wafer signifies the sacramental blood and body of Christ, and the process of his spiritual rebirth begins at this moment when the wafer-like sun appears in the sky. It is a symbol of salvation through death.

Robert Stallman, "Introduction" to The Red Badge of Courage, *1951*

If we were to seek a geometrical shape to picture the significant form of *The Red Badge*, it would not be the circle, the L, or the straight line of oscillation between selfishness and salvation, but the equilateral triangle. Its three points are instinct, ideals, and circumstance. Henry Fleming runs along the sides like a squirrel in a track. Ideals take him along one side until circumstance confronts him with danger. Then instinct takes over and he dashes down the third side in a panic. The panic abates somewhat as he approaches the angle of ideals, and as he turns the corner (continuing his flight) he busily rationalizes to accommodate those ideals. . . . Then he runs on to the line of circumstance, and he moves again toward instinct. He is always controlled on one line, along which he is both drawn and impelled by the two other forces.

Charles C. Walcutt, American Literary Naturalism: A Divided Stream, *1956*

Thus *The Red Badge of Courage,* which is something of a *tour de force* as a novel and which is chiefly noted for the advance it marks in the onset of realism on the American literary scene, is transmongrified into a religious allegory. . . . Observe, too, that the evidence for this thesis is drawn, not from a study of the narrative progression of Crane's novel as a whole, but from a single image and the amalgam of the initials of the tall soldier's name with the name of Jesus Christ. . . .

Philip Rahv, "Fiction and the Criticism of Fiction," 1956

Crane's magnum opus shows up the nature and value of courage. The heroic ideal is not what it has been claimed to be: so largely is it the product of instinctive responses to biological and traditional forces. But man does have will, and he has the ability to reflect, and though these do not guarantee that he can effect his own destiny, they do enable him to become responsible to some degree for the honesty of his personal vision.

Stanley B. Greenfield, "The Unmistakable Stephen Crane," 1958

THE AENEID
ALL QUIET ON THE WESTERN FRONT
ALL THE KING'S MEN
ANIMAL FARM
ANNA KARENINA
AS I LAY DYING
AS YOU LIKE IT
BABBIT
BEOWULF
BILLY BUDD & TYPEE
BRAVE NEW WORLD
CANDIDE
CANTERBURY TALES
CATCH-22
THE CATCHER IN THE RYE
CRIME AND PUNISHMENT
THE CRUCIBLE
CRY THE BELOVED COUNTRY
DAISY MILLER & TURN OF THE SCREW
DAVID COPPERFIELD
DEATH OF S SALESMAN
THE DIVINE COMEDY: THE INFERNO
DOCTOR FAUSTUS
DOLL'S HOUSE & HEDDA GABLER
DON QUIXOTE
ETHAN FROME
A FAREWELL TO ARMS
FAUST PARTS I AND II
FOR WHOM THE BELL TOLLS
THE GLASS MENAGERIE
   & STREET CAR NAMED DESIRE
THE GOOD EARTH
THE GRAPES OF WRATH
GREAT EXPECTATIONS
THE GREAT GATSBY
GULLIVER'S TRAVELS
HAMLET
HARD TIMES
THE HEART OF DARKNESS
 & THE SECRET SHARER
HENRY IV, PART I
THE HOUSE OF THE SEVEN GABLES
HUCKLEBERRY FINN
THE ILIAD
INVISIBLE MAN
JANE EYRE
JULIUS CAESAR
THE JUNGLE
KING LEAR
LIGHT IN AUGUST
LORD JIM
LORD OF THE FLIES

THE LORD OF THE RINGS
   & THE HOBBIT
MACBETH
MADAME BOVARY
THE MAYOR OF CASTERBRIDGE
THE MERCHANT OF VENICE
A MIDSUMMER NIGHT'S DREAM
MOBY DICK
MY ANTONIA
NATIVE SON
NEW TESTAMENT
1984
THE ODYSSEY
OEDIPUS TRILOGY
OF MICE AND MEN
THE OLD MAN AND THE SEA
OLD TESTAMENT
OLIVER TWIST
ONE FLEW OVER THE CUCKOO'S NEST
OTHELLO
OUR TOWN
PARADISE LOST
THE PEARL
PORTRAIT OF THE ARTIST
   AS A YOUNG MAN
PRIDE AND PREJUDICE
THE PRINCE
THE RED BADGE OF COURAGE
THE REPUBLIC
RETURN OF THE NATIVE
RICHARD III
ROMEO AND JULIET
THE SCARLET LETTER
A SEPARATE PEACE
SILAS MARNER
SLAUGHTERHOUSE FIVE
SONS AND LOVERS
THE SOUND AND THE FURY
STEPPENWOLF & SIDDHARTHA
THE STRANGER
THE SUN ALSO RISES
TALE OF TWO CITIES
THE TAMING OF THE SHREW
THE TEMPEST
TESS OF THE D'URBERVILLES
TO KILL A MOCKINGBIRD
TOM JONES
TOM SAWYER
TWELFTH NIGHT
WALDEN
WHO'S AFRAID OF VIRGINIA WOOLF?
WUTHERING HEIGHTS

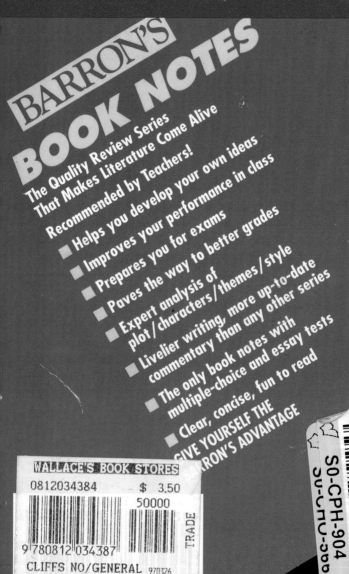

BARRON'S
BOOK NOTES

The Quality Review Series
That Makes Literature Come Alive
Recommended by Teachers!

- Helps you develop your own ideas
- Improves your performance in class
- Prepares you for exams
- Paves the way to better grades
- Expert analysis of plot/characters/themes/style
- Livelier writing, more up-to-date commentary than any other series
- The only book notes with multiple-choice and essay tests
- Clear, concise, fun to read

GIVE YOURSELF THE
BARRON'S ADVANTAGE

Margaret Atwood
In Search of
Alias Grace

Conférence Charles R. Bronfman

en Études canadiennes

Charles R. Bronfman Lecture

in Canadian Studies

LES PRESSES DE L'UNIVERSITÉ D'OTTAWA
UNIVERSITY OF OTTAWA PRESS